SURRENDER TO LEAD

MONICA HANNAN

SURRENDER TO LEAD

MONICA HANNAN

TLI
PUBLISHING
Phoenix, AZ

Contributors
Author: Monican Hannan
Preface: Fr. Basil Atwell, OSB
Reviewer: Mikaela Thom
Editor: Laurie Strom, TLI Publishing
Cover Design: Maria Fernanda Hernandez
Commentary: Cristofer Pereyra, Tepeyac Leadership, Inc.
Commentary: Most Reverend Thomas J. Olmsted,
                    Bishop Emeritus of Phoenix, AZ

Copyright © 2025 by TLI Publishing
www.TLIprogram.org
Phoenix

Scripture verses contained herein are from the New American Bible
Revised Edition, United States Conference of Catholic Bishops
(https://bible.usccb.org/bible)

ISBN: 979-8-9907711-3-0

Printed in the United States of America

Dedication

To my mother, who taught me how to pray, and no doubt prayed me back into the fold when I had other ideas. It's clear there's a great deal of power in a mother's appeals to God.

Hail Mary

"O Mother, strengthen the faith of our brothers and sisters in the laity, so that in every field of social, professional, cultural and political life, they may act in accordance with the truth and the law brought by your son to mankind." (Pope St. John Paul II 1979)

Acknowledgements

The Holy Spirit's timing can be fascinating. I received a phone call last fall from Tepeyac Leadership, Inc. CEO Cristofer Pereyra asking for a meeting to discuss a special project. I wasn't sure what was on his agenda, but it fit with mine because I planned to pitch a book idea to him. I wanted to feature his story in a book on servant leadership. At the meeting, he pitched his idea to me – asking if he could feature me in a book as part of the Tepeyac Leadership Series. We both laughed at the coincidence, then determined that neither one of us was interested in being the main focus of a book. Shortly after that meeting, though, I began to hear from people who had amazing surrender stories. It seemed to me as if the Holy Spirit was putting them in my path in all kinds of coincidental ways. It finally dawned on me that the book I was supposed to write was one that told those stories – and that's what this is.

The list of individuals who helped bring this book to completion is a long one, beginning with TLI CEO Cristofer Pereyra who has been an enthusiastic cheerleader for the project. Bishop Thomas Olmsted was a blessing, not only providing his insightful commentary but also making himself available time after time, even while on vacation. I want to thank Editor Laurie Strom, not only for her enormous skill in editing but for her clear-headed and diplomatic leadership and quick turnaround. Thanks also to Maria Fernanda Hernandez for the long hours spent creating the marvelous artwork for the book's cover – and not just one cover concept, but many. Mikaela Thom was the first to proofread the manuscript, and that's always a daunting task. Just figuring out where the commas shouldn't go can be a full-time job.

And most of all, a special thanks to the brave men and women who touched my soul – and hopefully yours – with their stories. Sharing at this level is not easy and can even be painful, but in the end, I trust their sacrifice will make a difference in the way people live and lead. God bless you all.

Table of Contents

Preface

Vulnerability doesn't come easily to many in today's social-media driven world. The perceived need to be better than the rest – to impress others while striving to get to the top in any given profession can take over one's life, no matter the cost. All of this striving to fit in is stealing away any hope of authenticity. It's very hard to allow ourselves to be seen as imperfect in a cancel culture, so we hide who we really are out of fear of being misunderstood or judged. We may congratulate ourselves on our hard-earned independence, when all the time, we're really dying on the inside of loneliness and alienation. One needs only to look at the rate of divorce and the statistics on troubled youth to see that society is in dire need of something more.

That something is the Triune God; and, in Divine Wisdom, God created Man to live not in isolation but in communion with others, as members of the Body of Christ. As Christendom has given way to secularism and society has devolved into separation and withdrawal, many have also decided they no longer need what has come to be derogatorily called "organized religion"; and the isolation continues to grow.

Given the modern situation, it's not hard to see why Pope Benedict XVI, in writing his Apostolic Letter, *Ubicumque et Semper,* expressed an urgent need for lay men and women to take a more active role in re-evangelizing those who have left the Church, while pointing out the challenges involved in spreading the gospel in this technological era, during a time when Christianity, as he put it, "has been particularly challenged by an abandonment of faith."

The Church is experiencing an urgent need for lay leaders who are willing to live out their faith authentically, evangelizing by how they do that – taking their values with them into their day-to-day – people who are willing to speak their truth without fear of being judged. A big part of that is surrendering to God's will.

The people who tell their stories here all experienced a surrender moment when they turned to God, often in distress, and gave themselves over to His will for their lives. The result for many has been unexpected. But it's also given them courage to be vulnerable.

At Assumption Abbey we live by the **Rule of St. Benedict.** This means we live in community, with our days centered on prayer and work. It's a Christ-centered existence that has worked for nearly 16 centuries. Ora et Labora. Prayer and Work. Our work, and God's work. Does this mean our lives are perfect? Not at all. But our visitors, when they arrive, tell us they can sense the peace that flourishes here. They spend a little time with us at Mass, communal prayer and shared meals, and then they head back out into their active lives, ready to take on the world once again. We Benedictines believe there is an important lesson there. We evangelize through our way of life. The visitor – be it a construction worker, a school teacher, a tourist, or a homeless man in need, whomever – is evangelized simply by how we live our lives in community through prayer and work. Ora et Labora.

As an oblate of St. Benedict, Monica Hannan prays with the Benedictine Community of Assumption Abbey twice a year; and, during the time we gather together in retreat, you can hear her asking a lot of questions. She's pretty good at getting people to open up and tell their stories. You'll find that to be true in this book. The stories will draw you in. And while you're immersed in these stories, perhaps you'll think of your own surrender moment and consider your own role in the New Evangelization.

Fr. Basil Atwell, OSB

Introduction

"Few souls understand what God would accomplish in them if they were to abandon themselves unreservedly to Him and if they were to allow His grace to mold them accordingly."

~ St. Ignatius of Loyola

When the phone rings in the middle of the night, it's rarely good news. I was six years old when my mother answered that call. She'd been pacing anyway, wondering why my father was so late coming home. Lateness wasn't unusual for him. He was a salesman who often worked well past dinnertime. Many nights, my mother kept his meal warm while we waited. But on this night, he was exceptionally late. The year was 1966, long before cellphones, so all she could do was worry. I had been in bed for hours already, but I wasn't asleep. Anxiety was in the air, which is perhaps one of the reasons I remember it so well. I heard her voice as she answered the first call, and then she made another. I padded out to the kitchen, and she saw me just standing there, saying nothing.

"Go back to bed," she said in that too-calm voice that children everywhere understand means "be on high alert." I didn't obey but continued to watch her. Finally, she relented and said, "Daddy's been in an accident, but everything's all right. Now go to sleep."

3

She didn't really know that everything was all right. My father had been driving home on a dark, winding road and apparently fell asleep at the wheel. He left the road and slammed into a ditch hard enough to be thrown through the windshield of his white Volkswagen station wagon. He was a big man, over 200 pounds, and that windshield was small. The pressure of the crash must have been intense. He went face-first and had head trauma, but his most severe injuries were caused by the stem of the rearview mirror. The sharp remainder of what hadn't broken off on his fly-by had acted like a knife, slicing into his leg.

The call my mother received was from the emergency room doctor, who told her about the accident and that, blessedly, my father had been alone in the car. The paramedics who brought him in said no other vehicles were involved. He was badly banged up but was expected to survive. The second call, the one my mother made, was to my uncle. As my mother remembers it, "I had small children at home, I didn't drive. So, I called your Uncle Bob to go to the hospital to be with him."

My dad came home on Halloween night, appropriate for the way he looked—his face a mass of purple and yellow bruises, his leg a mess, but healing. He did recover.

The events of that night did not change his behavior, but they did impact mine. After that, whenever he was late coming home, I would go into my room and kneel by my bed, praying to Jesus with great intensity, asking that Dad make it home safely. Most nights, I would remain on my knees until I heard his car in the driveway, and only then would I climb into bed with a great sense of relief. It is my earliest memory of turning to God in a time of need, with total belief that my prayer was heard. I think I felt that as long as I kept praying, he would be safe, and from what I could see, it always worked. This was my routine for years.

I'd like to say that this total dependence on God continued as I grew up, but as I got older, a distance developed. Like all good Catholic mothers, mine did her best to instill her faith. She saw to it that I attended Catholic school when it was available, that I learned my

4

catechism, and that I received First Communion and Confirmation. In junior high, I was drawn to Young Life and Christian clubs, but that was more for the inclusion than by any real sense of faith or worship.

By high school, the busyness of life took over, and I began what would become a long slide away. I became the kind of Catholic who fulfills obligations. I married a Catholic, we raised our children Catholic, and we also made sure they attended Catholic school, but suffice it to say, I was in the middle of a decades-long period of public participation but private spiritual drought.

Fortunately for me, Jesus never gives up, and here's how He caught me. Again, it was through my dad. Subsequent mishaps and hard living didn't kill him, and neither did his later battles with cancer or heart disease. But by the time he was well into his 80s, he was finally slowing down, and he sensed that death was knocking at the door. He had always been afraid of the idea of dying, and I wanted to help him with that. While he wasn't comfortable talking about it, he was my biggest fan, and I knew that if I wrote a book, he would read it. So, I began researching comforting stories on death and dying. I interviewed dozens of people who had near-death stories—those who work with the dying, those who had stories of loved ones who had beautiful deathbed experiences—and I tied those to traditional Catholic beliefs.

While I was doing that research, I was relearning a lot of things I had forgotten about my own faith, and perhaps most importantly, I had begun to relearn how to pray. I signed up for a regular timeslot in Eucharist Adoration. To this day, I'm not sure what compelled me to do that. Sitting still long enough to do anything is very hard for me. Sitting still while praying was at first almost impossible, but that's a story for another time. I can only say, looking back, that the prayers were working in ways that only the Holy Spirit could see.

Sadly, before I finished the book, my dad died. But that, too, became an important part of the book. Once I had finished it, I began speaking about the topic of death and dying, mainly to Catholic groups, but nearly always to faith groups. I thought at the time that it would be a second career path for me. I hired a publicist and began to expand my social media presence, doing all the things a speaker does to get my name out there. At the same time, my publicist thought I would have more credibility as a speaker if I had a subject-related degree behind my name, as many speakers do on specific topics. With that in mind, I enrolled in the Augustine Institute in Denver and began my studies for a master's degree in theology. I have always been a big fan of education, and the topic itself was of interest, so it wasn't a hard sell.

All was going according to plan, and then Covid hit. Like so many things during those pandemic lockdown months, my plans came to a screeching halt. I did get the degree during that time, but like everybody else, I was stuck in a bubble, and my momentum fell to zero. My faith had grown strong, and I now had a firm grounding in the history and teachings of the Church. But as the pandemic ended, I was faced with the prospect of either starting over to build a following or just letting it go, and the latter is what I decided to do.

It was a surrender moment. I simply chose to wait, to turn my life over to God and let Him decide what I should do with it. I remember thinking that perhaps all my writing and education had been meant for me alone. All those long nights of study had certainly gone a long way toward my own salvation, so in that way, they were invaluable.

I put my attention back into my job as a managing editor at a television station in the upper Midwest, mentoring young reporters and anchors, all the while attending daily Mass, going to Adoration, and nurturing my prayer life. There was one difference. Where before I had never talked about my Catholic faith at work, now everybody knew I was Catholic. I wasn't afraid to make the Sign of the Cross at the lunch table, for instance, or mention that I had just come from Mass—subtle things.

"Just so, your light must shine before others" – Matthew 5:16

It's hard to imagine a more secular business than television news. We're supposed to be neutral; that's the goal. But let's be honest: because we're human, nobody is ever truly neutral, and over the years, political leanings have made television news a business where networks tend to unapologetically choose sides. On a local level, that's happening more slowly, but young reporters have been influenced by societal messages to such a degree that they often can't recognize bias even when it's pointed out to them. It influences what is covered and how it's covered, and journalists who claim it doesn't are kidding themselves. I worked for much of my career in a more balanced office than some, but still, there had been moments in my career when I felt my news judgment was questioned because a news manager knew of my Catholic faith.

But something changed. One Ash Wednesday not long ago, I walked into the newsroom, looked around, and saw ashes on the foreheads of at least two-thirds of the young people in the room. It was such an awakening moment for me. What courage they had! Even the young anchors wore their ashes as they read the news, and nobody said a word. Perhaps this is a single good that has come out of the "wokeism" that pervades society today—the idea that we feel we can be who we are at work, and nobody feels they have a right to question it, at least when it comes to faith as it influences our personal appearance. In any event, I realized at that moment that these young people are leaders in their faith without even trying; they are young evangelists simply by their actions.

Shortly thereafter, out of the blue, I received a message on LinkedIn from Cristofer Pereyra with an organization called Tepeyac Leadership Initiative (TLI) asking for a meeting. I had never heard of the group or of Cristofer. Normally, I would have ignored it, but again, for reasons I can't explain, I said yes. He had reached out because he was looking for a broadcast journalist to speak to a group of TLI participants about the media, and I agreed. I did that for two years, after which Cristofer asked me to serve on his advisory board. Looking to expand into the upper Midwest, he subsequently asked me to serve on the TLI national board. I can't help but wonder if this has been God's purpose all along, and maybe I would never have known it had I not finally given up my own plans and opened myself up to His plans for me. I discussed this with Most Reverend Thomas J. Olmsted, Bishop Emeritus of Phoenix, AZ, and one of the founders of TLI. He said he hadn't planned on starting the program that became TLI either. His plan was to identify Hispanic leaders among the faithful in the Phoenix Diocese, but he quickly discovered that there was a need to develop leaders from all backgrounds. From that modest beginning, Tepeyac Leadership Initiative quickly grew into an international lay leadership program in less than a decade.

"We need not know 'when' He is at work in us or 'when' He is at work in others," Bishop Olmsted reminded me. "Jesus makes all things work together for the good; let us leave it all in His hands."

The stories I share here are of people who have learned how to do that, and the grace that has flowed into their often difficult lives has been a direct result of their ultimate surrender. At the same time, TLI's mission is about forming lay leaders, and that story is here as well.

Chapter One

"If we let Christ into our lives, we lose nothing, nothing, absolutely nothing of what makes life free, beautiful, and great. No! Only in this friendship are the doors of life opened wide. Only in this friendship is the great potential of human existence truly revealed."

~ Pope Benedict XVI

Every pope in the last 150 years has had something to say about surrendering to Christ, and it's likely a fair assumption that faith leaders all the way back to St. Peter would say the same. There are so many things that hold us back, not the least of which is pride. We get hung up on the idea that we need to handle things by ourselves. We often see doing otherwise as a sign of weakness. The unfortunate result is typically loneliness and unrequited longing. We may not know what we long for, but that sense of dissatisfaction hovers in our soul, looking for something to fill it. Some try to satisfy it with alcohol or drugs. The high we may get from substances or from new relationships or career successes may distract us for a while; some people shop for things they don't need or take elaborate trips—whatever we have to do to fill the void. These things never quite hit the mark, and we're left still looking for that next big thing that will satisfy our longing.

The answer to our quest, of course, is God. He wrote our desire for union with Him into our life code, and when we don't have that union, we can't truly be at peace. So strong is this belief that it is written into the Catholic Catechism as a tenet of the Faith.

"The desire for God is written in the human heart, because man is created by God and for God; and God never ceases to draw man to himself. Only in God will he find the truth and happiness he never stops searching for." – CCC 27

The Catechism goes on to explain that man has searched for God from the beginning of time, and it's only in the present age that the cult of the "nones" has begun to proliferate. But just because a person does not espouse any particular faith or belief in God does not mean they are not still seeking Him. Modern scientists have published recent work that seems to suggest what the Church has always known, that this search is written into human DNA. One can debate how it got there, whether put there by a higher being or as a mode of survival, but increasingly, researchers believe it exists. For people of faith, there is only one explanation. God continues reaching out to those He has created. He intends for His people to be sharers in Christ's life and to take up their roles as priests, prophets, and kings.

Of course, it's a role we can't properly carry out if we don't get control over ourselves and rule over our own sin. But Jesus tells us He never gives up on us, even when we ignore Him or try to get by on our own power. Too often, as Jonathan Marohl discovered, it takes a crisis to bring us to our senses.

"Because I know that you are stubborn and that your neck is an iron sinew and your forehead bronze" – Isaiah 48:4

Cowboys tend to meet certain characteristics. They're known to be tough, independent, and stubborn. Jonathan Marohl never wanted to be anything but a cowboy. The son of a Vietnam vet who served on the front lines, he will tell you his life as a child was not always predictable, and while he doesn't like to go into detail, it's clear there is some pain there. Still, what he learned growing up on a small farm in Minnesota set him up for a life that he grew to love.

"I just absolutely loved cows and horses and rodeos. It's all I dreamed of, owning my own ranch someday," he said.

His mother was Catholic and saw to it that he learned the faith in childhood, giving him a firm foundation.

"My mom came from a strong Catholic family, and so growing up, we went to Mass every Sunday. It wasn't an option," he said.

He admits church was more of a chore than a love in those early days. But in high school, he joined a youth group that he credits with helping to shape who he's become as an adult.

Jonathan maintained his Mass habit in college. He studied animal and range science at North Dakota State University and, after marriage, bought his own ranch on the outskirts of the rugged Badlands where he and his wife began raising their family. He was on the path to success as a rancher and a businessman, and as his children came along, he became increasingly busy. While he was highly successful in his career, internally, he was conflicted.

"On the outside, I was a strong, confident, outgoing, fun-loving, hardworking guy," he said, "but on the inside, I was really struggling with a lot of things. I was able to mask it, I guess, suppress it."

That's when he got his first wake-up call from God.

"We had rented some ground up west of Minot [North Dakota] to run some cows, and I went up there one day to move cattle and doctor any that were sick," Jonathan said.

He had finished his work for the day and was heading back to the corrals.

"I'd had some frustrating moments that afternoon," he recalled, "and I wasn't behaving as I should, let's just say that. So, I was loping the horse back, and there's this tall grass everywhere, and he stepped in a badger hole and went down. The first thing that hit the ground was my head, and the horse landed on top of me. The second my head hit the ground, I just heard God speak to me, and He said, 'Knock it off!'"

Jonathan said he knew just what God meant. "I knew exactly what he was talking about. The struggles in my life, the sins that I had. I knew then that I needed to get a grip on myself and get rid of them."

On his way home, he called his parish priest and shared what had happened and went to Confession right then and there. For most people, that wake-up call may have been enough. But as Jonathan said, he's stubborn. He said he was putting a great deal of effort into changing, but he was trying to do all the work himself. It hadn't occurred to him to ask God for help. Another three years went by, "and I still wasn't any better," he said.

In his work life, though, things continued to go well. In addition to his ranch life, Jonathan had taken on a full-time job in the animal health industry. He was traveling a lot, but it paid well, he had a company vehicle and retirement benefits—things ranchers can't always depend on.

"It was the greatest job I'd ever had in my life," he said. "I didn't know there could be a job that good."

As his success grew, he was assigned to different marketing committees around the country and was starting to do sales training for new hires, all of which involved travel—and that was the problem. It was pulling him away from his young family.

"I could tell my kids needed me. My boys were getting to an age where they needed their dad around more. As a young man, I had promised myself that if I ever had a family, I would be the best dad and father I could, and I could see that I was drawn away from them for the pursuit of money and success. So, I decided to walk away from it all. It was a big turning point for me," a turning point, he said, in that he put that drive into working more for the Lord, and for his family.

"That was the first time I went to Cursillo [a Catholic retreat]. I went there not really knowing what it was, but I had just a fantastic encounter with God, just in terms of trust. I had walked away from a great job, and I was just relying on Him to provide," he said.

He began working on a ranch closer to home, and family life improved. But at the same time, he said he was still facing the same old struggles. He was working with cow-calf pairs on a ranch in South Dakota, but still living on his ranch near St. Anthony, North Dakota. He would get up early, load up his horses, and drive to the ranch, work there, and then drive home. He thought things were going pretty well. But then he received his second wake-up call.

"I got up, it was probably about 3:00 in the morning, and I got the horses caught and saddled and ready and took off and went down there. And I was down there by 5:30 in the morning, and the sun was just coming up," he said.

Jonathan said there were sick cows that needed attention, and he and another rancher spent the day doctoring them.

"I was just in absolute heaven. It was like the greatest thing for me. It was a beautiful place. Right along the river, there's big cottonwood trees all over and grass, and just like my ideal thing. So, it was in the afternoon, and it was kind of getting hot. We just had a few more calves to try to catch and treat. There was one that was just starting to get sick, and he was hanging in the rear. So, I really wanted to get to him. We were there to do a job, and I was going to get them all done no matter what. He

13

was pretty quick. So, he took off running. At the time, I was riding my fastest horse, named Buckwheat. He's a big buckskin. We got this calf out of the trees. He crossed the river, went down the other side. So, we crossed the river and got up on this flat. There's a big prairie dog town up there. I just spurred the horse and took off and got right on top of that calf, and we were going wide open, and I was just leaning forward and getting ready to rope this calf. And right before I threw my rope, the horse stepped in a prairie dog hole, and we came crashing down. Same thing. The first thing that hit was my neck and my left shoulder, and then the horse was on top of me. I was still in the saddle. I had both feet in the stirrups. I heard a loud pop when I hit the ground. And for a second time, God spoke to me, and he just said, 'Knock it off!' It was so clear and so piercing. Anyway, I kicked my feet out of the stirrups and the horse got up and just stood there."

Jonathan said it took him a while to get up off the ground. He knew he was hurt, but at first, he didn't realize just how badly. He was a long way from anything and felt there was no other option but to get himself back up on that horse, which he eventually forced himself to do. He rode back to the pickup, got the horses back to the ranch, took care of their needs, and drove home. The experience of hearing God's voice impacted him profoundly, so once again, on the way home, he called his parish priest, who met him on the highway and again heard his confession.

"Because I was so open and vulnerable, it was the greatest confession I ever made," he admitted. "My pain was intense. But as soon as I started the confession, all my pain went away. It was like I was floating through the entire confession. I felt so much peace and so much love. And then I drove home."

He said when he walked in the door, his wife took one look at him and said, "What happened to you?!"

"I said I got a little dinged up," he told me with a smile.

Just so you know what a cowboy's version of "a little dinged up" actually is, here's a rundown of his injuries. When the horse fell on him, Jonathan suffered a broken collarbone that split vertically, from one end to the other. He also had a separated shoulder, broken ribs, and a concussion. And with all of that, he still rode a horse, drove a truck, did the chores necessary to make sure the horses were taken care of, and he even saw to his own soul, all before sitting down in a chair. But once he did sit down, he found it difficult to get up again. He took nothing for the pain, but instead, did what his mother had always suggested when something hurt. He offered it up. He spent two days in that chair before his wife finally insisted that he go to a doctor, who looked him over, then ordered surgery to repair what he'd broken. But before all that, as he sat in that chair, he had another profound experience.

"It was early in the morning, and I was in a lot of pain. Suddenly, the pain went away. Jesus appeared on the left-hand side and Mary and John the Baptist appeared on the right-hand side of our living room. Their backs were toward me. But they were there, and they were distinctly each of those individuals. There was no question in my mind. Nothing was said. They were just there. A few moments went by, and they just faded away. And then, on the wall in big, bold, black letters were the words 'John 5:6.' I couldn't even get out of the chair by myself. But the next morning, when my wife woke up, I asked her to get my Bible, and I looked it up. It was the story where there was a man who was sitting by the pool at Bethesda, and he was 38 years old. And the interesting thing was, I was 38 years old. And Jesus asks him, 'Do you want to be healed?' And so, that was His question for me. I'd been trying my whole life to do things on my own. I'd worked hard, stayed busy, made money—all working towards a dream. But it was in that moment where He asked me if I wanted to be healed. I didn't answer right away. It took me a couple days. I was taking the same work ethic from the world into my spiritual life up to that point— that if I can just work hard enough, I can eventually rid myself of all these sins. But finally, I said 'Yes, I want to be healed,' and then I wept. So much hurt and pain and history were just coming

15

out. It was so relieving. And since that moment, I have not failed in the major things."

Still, he said it did take him some time to get to the point in his life where he was able to understand why he needed to fall off that horse.

"There are benefits to having a lot of self-confidence and being able to deal with stuff and handle pain. A lot of the characteristics that make up cowboys are fantastic, but at the same time, they can be really hard to overcome," he said. "And like the spiritual life, you've got to surrender. Well, surrender's not really a word that I'd ever used in my life, because I just associated that with weakness."

"Trust in the Lord with all your heart,
and on your own intelligence do not rely" – Proverbs 3:5

In 2023, he attended the Eucharistic Congress in Indianapolis, and there he had a third profound experience that finally allowed him to come to terms with the concept of surrender and to understand the source of his struggle.

"One of the evenings, there was the Eucharistic procession that came in Lucas Oil Stadium. All the lights are off, and there's this huge monstrance and all these priests, and they're processing, and they went through this litany of forgiveness. And at the end of that, there I was in the very highest top section of the stadium, Section 440, kneeling on the concrete floor, and I just started saying I was sorry. And it was louder and louder, and there's people around me, and I didn't care, and I just kept saying it. And again, He came to me. I just closed my eyes, and He took me back to the time of my life where the root of all my sins started, and He let me just dwell there. And then I saw His hand come into my soul. And just with two fingers, He just reached in and grabbed it and then just

16

lifted it and removed it. I could feel it. Every single thing was just released. Since then, it has sparked a fire and a desire to share this with other people and encourage them and tell them, 'Whatever you're dealing with, you can do it. Nothing is impossible with God.'"

The experience of healing took years, and learning to surrender to the will of God took even longer, but at the age of 46, Jonathan decided to enroll in Tepeyac Leadership Initiative to learn how to better lead others to Christ. In his business of selling agricultural products or helping with cattle drives, he's able to witness to a group of people who tend to be just like him—a stubborn and private lot of cowboys who would rather be crushed by a horse than admit they are in need.

"That's the thing about surrender," he said. "To do it, we have to overcome selfishness, which comes naturally. It's when we say no to ourselves first that we can begin to overcome that."

That means saying no to technology, pornography, the lure of money, addictions, infidelities—whatever it is that takes you away from time spent with God and with family and from those responsibilities you know you should be focused on.

"What I'm learning is that good leaders, through their example and their invitation, can encourage others to surrender. I'm kind of a slow learner, and God had to use force to get me to my low points to actually listen to Him," he said.

But he hopes he can help to get the message through with a little less force for others, simply by being there and being willing to share his story and his faith.

"I have been so stubborn and hard-headed and selfish," he said. "I have rejected God, I have run from Him, I have pursued other things. It took some major experiences and getting my bell rung before I was ready to surrender to God, but I did and praise the Lord."

17

Chapter Two

"We shall find it difficult to estimate the moral power which a single individual, trained to practice what he teaches, may acquire in his own circle, in the course of years."

~ *St. John Henry Newman*

Jesus tasked His disciples with evangelizing the entire world, and it worked. Christianity spread so fast among the ancients that there could be no argument that the Holy Spirit was with the believers, aiding them in their mission. So, how can we explain today's circumstances? There's no doubt we are living in a post-Christian era, a time when our society and our ethics have been shaped by 2,000 years of Christian culture, but people increasingly identify themselves as either spiritual but non-religious, or as agnostic, or even as atheist.

It's not a new phenomenon. Religious scholars can't place the blame on any one thing, but rather on a whole host of societal events and changes, beginning with the so-called Enlightenment that began in the 17th Century, when Liberalism steadily grew into what we call Relativism today. All forms of media have worked together to convince many that the greatest sin they can commit today is to judge others, with the result being an entire generation of individuals who live by the standard that says, "It may not be right for me, but who am I to judge you?" Along with that comes the conviction that there's no definitive truth in religion; that it's all a matter of personal opinion.

When the framers of Vatican II gave lay Catholics their marching orders, they meant to combat this shift that had been happening for years, but it was a message that was largely missed at the time.

"The major call, it seems to me, of the Church is the main document, *Lumen Gentium*, which is the call to holiness," Bishop Olmsted explained. "But it got put on the back burner because of liturgical issues. Historically, I think that was impacted because after the Second World War, up until the time of the Second Vatican Council, we had liturgical commissions within the United States, groups that were doing education of the laity among us for the sacred liturgy. A lot of times, we relied on them rather than on the bishops themselves to pass on what the Church was teaching. So, the emphasis in the beginning, in the first number of years after the Council, was more on liturgy than on impacting society by a real lived faith. I also think the impact of the sexual revolution did a lot of damage in the cultural sense, in particular."

The answer to that, he said, came later from Pope St. John Paul II when he wrote *The Theology of the Body*, which offered Catholics an understanding of the complementarity between men and women.

"We needed an articulation of that to help us move more confidently forward in living with what the Second Vatican Council called for in terms of holiness in the home, holiness in our place of work, and holiness in the culture," Bishop Olmsted said.

John Paul II warned Catholics against two temptations: first, to become so involved in their parishes that they would fail to take the message out into the secular world; and second, to consider their faith lives and their day-to-day lives as separate. That's certainly not how the early disciples spread Christianity in the world. Instead, John Paul II rallied the troops, calling for a New Evangelization—one that lay Catholics could no longer ignore.

It wasn't really new; it was based on the words of Christ himself and echoed by Church leaders and saints down through the ages, asking faithful believers to take their sincere and well-grounded message out to their communities, leading others to Christ through example and firm commitment.

"Lay leaders bring their faith into all sectors of culture and society," said Bishop Olmsted. "As they engage in temporal affairs, they receive the grace and mission to 'order them according to the plan of God' (Lumen Gentium, 31). It was said of Servant of God Dorothy Day: 'She lived as though the truth were true!' Even when unwelcomed by some, her words planted seeds of hope for the poor, the unemployed, and the unwanted."

St. John Henry Newman believed in the power of personal influence as the best source of evangelization. He wrote, "It persuades the weak, the timid, the wavering, and the inquiring."

But it's tough to do if you're convinced you don't need God or religion because you've got the world by the tail.

What Do You Do When You Discover You Aren't Invincible After All?

Ask Christian Ford if he's ever been in a life and death situation, and at first, he'll downplay it. He spent nearly a decade among the Navy elite, most of it as a Navy SEAL, so the training alone was dangerous, never mind the missions themselves. He's reticent to go into detail about much of what he did during his time in the SEALs, one of the youngest in the community at the time, except to say that the life of a SEAL is intense and often painful, and that everything you hear about the toughness of the training is true, because these servicemen are the best of the best. They have to be just to survive.

"When you say, 'Did I ever do anything where my life was in danger?' I mean, you do that continuously," he explained. "Your life is always in danger; you're boarding ships in the middle of the night to get up on a large container ship. You're out on the sea, it's cold, there are currents. We had guys get crushing knee injuries. I knew a guy who broke his back, but I didn't have a broken leg or anything like that."

Except, he *did* have back injuries, and then there was the time a diversionary grenade exploded on his right foot, breaking the metatarsals and putting him in a cast.

"They wanted me in it for eight weeks, but I made them take it off after three," he said.

And once during training, he suffered an episode of O_2 toxicity during a dive in water that was around 40 degrees Fahrenheit. He doesn't really remember much of what happened there, because he blacked out briefly until his swim buddy got him to the surface. But he said that's always a risk when you're using an oxygen rebreather (an apparatus that absorbs carbon dioxide and replenishes oxygen, allowing divers to remain under water longer). Because that kind of training dive is routine, he doesn't really count that as life-threatening. He stopped to think.

"Well, I did have a parachute malfunction that was interesting," he said.

He went on to describe a free-fall jump during a training exercise. The weather was good, there was no wind, and everything looked great. At 12,000 feet, when he made the jump, things looked normal. He was in position with the other team members around him. When it was time to do the wave off—a visual signal to the others that he was about to open his parachute—that's when the trouble started.

"I smelled black powder," he remembered. "That was my reserve. There's a little device in the reserve parachute that, based on pressure, will automatically deploy. So, mine malfunctioned, basically. It deployed when it wasn't supposed to."

Two parachutes seem like it would be twice as good, but Christian explained that is not the case, because as the reserve starts to get air, it can wrap around the main chute, and both parachutes will become tangled and useless.

"I looked over my right shoulder and could see that the main chute was fully deployed so I wasn't going very fast, and I could see the reserve was kind of flapping around, but I could tell it wanted to inflate under the main, and [if it did] there was the potential for the two to get wrapped up," he explained.

He said it was a scenario that SEALs train for, and in theory, Christian knew what to do, but having the presence of mind to follow the necessary steps took intense concentration as well as a whole lot of nerve. He acknowledged that most people would panic in this situation.

"I was very focused, but you definitely get that fight or flight sensation. It's at this point that the training kicked in. I was able to get my hand up and hold the risers and kind of push them down enough before cutting away the main chute... and hope the reserve inflated enough so that I could ride it in. I reached over and saw the reserve wasn't inflating. So now it's like, 'Well, I'm going to have to place all my chips on a partially inflated reserve and get rid of a good parachute,'" he said.

While all that was happening, Christian's attention was focused skyward rather than on the ground, so he wasn't paying attention to his altitude or the direction he was headed. Normally, he would have been steering toward a landing zone, but on this occasion, his priority was to get one of the parachutes to safely inflate while letting the other one go.

"I had my hand up, pulled the reserve down, released the main, and I kind of dropped and swung like a pendulum a little bit, and the reserve finally did inflate," he remembered. "And then I looked down and realized I was coming in fast, and there was the tree line! I thought, 'Well, great. Now I'm going to come in at 25 miles an hour, and I'm going to smack the trees.' I was able to clear them, but to do so, I had to make a downwind landing. It doesn't take a lot of wind to make a downwind landing... uh... unpleasant.

"I crashed into the ground. I hit really hard. Fortunately for me, it had rained a couple days prior, so the ground was still soft, and it sucked one of my boots off. I got dragged a bit, and I was lying there wondering what I had snapped. You know how you kind of do that self-check? And miraculously, I didn't have any major injuries, although I could tell I was going to be pretty sore. That's the beauty of being in your 20s. If I took that landing today, I'd be in traction for six months," he added with a laugh.

Christian readily admits that the training he received in the SEALs and his escape from a variety of near misses gave him a sense of his own invincibility. But looking back now, he recognizes that from a faith standpoint, he was lost.

"You know, when I was driving my Ninja at 130 miles an hour on I-15 in San Diego, drunk, those were times when I was drifting way out at sea. People who do that kind of work, who can maintain a strong faith, I really admire, because once you go through that training, you feel invincible. It's very easy to feel like, 'I don't need that. I'm good to go.' You feel like you could accomplish anything. What usually happens is you have some kind of a wake-up call," he said.

That wake-up call didn't happen right away. Instead, for Christian, the successes kept happening, one after another. When he left the SEALs, he went on to university for a political science degree, followed by a master's degree from Yale in international relations and then a law degree from the University of California, Berkeley. He even studied for a PhD, all while raising a young family with his wife, Amy. With experience working at the Department of Homeland Security and time spent in private practice, he was approached to work at the Department of Defense, so the family moved back to Washington, D.C., where they would spend the next 10 years as he moved up the ladder of success. The end of the first Trump Administration found him working as a Deputy

Assistant Attorney General under Attorney General William Barr—a job that would end when the administration ended.

Suddenly and almost without warning, after all he had accomplished in his work life, Christian hit a wall that he couldn't seem to climb.

"It was a very challenging time to be on the job market," he explained. "There was a lot of uncertainty about the economy. There were still concerns about Covid. I think the political climate was very challenging as well."

Because of the sharp political divide in the country, Christian found that his decision to work in the previous administration seemed to be an impediment—something that he hadn't expected.

"I had worked on national security issues. That area tends not to change dramatically from administration to administration, and I worked with people on both sides of the political aisle," he explained. "It was always professional and cordial, so it was kind of a shock to me how some legal professionals on the outside viewed it. There were a lot of misunderstandings—how I landed in that position and why I landed in that position. I thought, 'Why am I being punished for policies and ideologies that are associated with other people that I didn't work with?' I had never had someone flat out say, 'Because of your government service, we're not going to hire you.'"

Eight long months passed with interview after interview. Now he knows that the time frame isn't all that unusual for someone looking for a job in corporate law, but at the time, Christian worried that he wouldn't be able to provide for his family. For the first time in his life, he felt as if he wasn't in control, and it scared and depressed him.

Having been raised Catholic by his devout parents, and like so many Catholics, he had gone to Sunday Mass as an adult out of a sense of obligation over the years, especially raising his young family, but about a month into his job search, he began attending daily Mass, somewhat out of desperation.

"I'd go in there every day like a lot of us do when we're in need, and you're asking, 'Hey God, help me to do this' or 'help me do that, help me to find a place to land. Make this happen.' And you know, it takes a long time for some of us to realize that's not really the right thing to ask," he said.

He admits it was a surrender moment.

"I finally just realized I couldn't keep pounding my head against the wall. I thought, 'You know what? I don't think I'm going about this in the right way,'" he said.

It was at that point that the context of his prayers changed.

"Now it was, 'Help me to do your will. Whatever I'm supposed to do, just let me know.' I decided I'm just going to put it in God's hands," he recalled.

Just three days later, he received a good job offer, and he hasn't looked back.

He will also tell you he's changed from that young man who needlessly risked his life on a California highway. He doesn't pull any punches about that time in his life, which he said both helped him and had the potential to lead to an early death.

"I was one pothole away from dying. I lost teammates," he admitted.

He said the training that the military gives to SEALs is almost too good.

"The country should be really impressed and proud that we can produce those warriors. People who are not afraid to take huge risks," he added. "We hope those risks will be limited to critical situations for national security or the battlefield, but that's not the way humans work.

Once you create someone like that and condition someone to take on that level of risk, especially young people like me at the time, they're more likely to live high-risk lifestyles both in their off-duty lives and on the battlefield. It's hard to be safe and cautious in your personal life and be a warrior who's willing to run toward danger."

Christian said he does wonder why some teammates died and he didn't when they were taking such huge risks, but he has a theory.

"If I had a special task I am supposed to perform, I don't know what that is. But I do believe now in the power of prayer, that there's something to that. There were a lot of people praying for me. I know my family was praying for me, my parents were. I was really lucky to have that security net because I was pushing the envelope," he said.

Sometimes God answers those prayers through the people He puts in your path, and for Christian, one of those people was a philosophy instructor, a Vietnam veteran, who saw something in him that he hadn't even seen in himself.

"She said, 'You really need to think about going to school.' So, I did, I started thinking about it, and that's when I thought, 'You know, I'm ready to try something else,'" he recalled.

Looking at his academic resume, it may seem as if it was an easy decision, but he said he had to give up a lot in leaving the SEAL team, because he'd put his heart and soul into it.

"I was still enjoying jumping out of airplanes—jumping above the clouds at night. I still enjoyed shooting guns. I loved my teammates. They were the highest performing, highest caliber group of people you'll ever work with in your life. There's just nothing like it. I gave up a lot to walk away from it. But somehow, it all worked out. The fact that I had a burning desire all of a sudden to get out and go to college... well... if you don't believe in Divine Intervention, it seems unexplainable," he said.

At the same time, he said his military training helped him in his life and career after he left the Navy. It taught him what it feels like to push himself beyond what he thought his limits were.

"Once you do that, you realize that your preexisting notions of what you can and can't do are probably not accurate," he said. "When you're motivated, when you're committed, when you have the passion to do something, more often than not, you're going to exceed what you think those limitations are. There are people in life—I've met them—who've experienced that, who think, 'I can only go this far,' yet somehow went beyond that line and realized, 'Wow! I have more potential than I thought. I can do more than I thought I could do.' When you have that kind of reference point, it really empowers you. You don't have to run 15 miles on a beach. It can apply to life. It can apply to raising your family or challenges at work."

Today, Christian takes on leadership roles in his professional life, but he doesn't do it alone. He invites God into his daily decisions. He starts his day with a Rosary, and he said he takes the time every morning as a matter of discipline to reflect on the day, or as he puts it, to find his "spiritual sea legs."

"I say, 'Whatever your will is, just let me know. I'm going to power on and do what I need to do during the day, but feel free to let me know if something I'm doing is not consistent with your will.' I think servant leadership is understanding that there's a higher calling than yourself," he said. "It's really another way of describing humility. Some of the best leaders I've ever worked for were so good because they were humble. They just wanted to get the right answer. They were confident enough to go to subordinates, to go to other people to say, 'What do you think the right answer is?' In some ways, people will spin that as a lack of confidence, but I see that as complete confidence. And it also suggests that someone has a higher calling. They're not just focused on themselves.

"As humans, especially in the business world, you're always getting pushed and pulled in different directions—morally, legally, you have to stand your ground, and sometimes you have to resist the easy way and take the hard way. Sometimes that's reaching out to someone who you absolutely don't want to talk to, maybe you're convinced they don't like you, or they want to undermine what you're trying to do. It's that little voice that tells you to reach out and connect with them, because either you're misunderstanding the situation, or if you're not, by reaching out, you're going to improve the situation by showing grace and forgiveness."

Christian has always been a leader: from high school sports to time spent on a Navy SEAL Team to working in the halls of power with the U.S. Attorney General to helping clients while working in international law. But he has learned there's a difference between leading because that's what you've been hired or trained to do, and leading because that's where God has put you. The road may not be easy, and sometimes the only thing to do is wait, but in the words of Pope St. John Paul II, "The way Jesus shows you is not easy. Rather, it is like a path winding up a mountain... The steeper the road, the faster it rises toward ever wider horizons."

Chapter Three

"Many, even among the authorities, believed in him, but because of the Pharisees they did not acknowledge it openly in order not to be expelled from the synagogue."

~ John 12:42

It takes great courage to stand up in the public square and risk the anger of one's contemporaries. People have never taken kindly to having their views challenged. St. Paul even boasted of it:

> *"Are they servants of Christ? —I am speaking as if insane—I more so; in far more labors, in far more imprisonments, beaten times without number, often in danger of death. Five times I received from the Jews thirty-nine lashes. Three times I was beaten with rods, once I was stoned, three times I was shipwrecked, a night and a day I have spent adrift at sea. I have been on frequent journeys, in dangers from rivers, dangers from robbers, dangers from my countrymen, dangers from the Gentiles, dangers in the city, dangers in the wilderness, dangers at sea, dangers among false brothers. I have been in labor and hardship, through many sleepless nights, in hunger and thirst, often without food, in cold and exposure." – 2 Corinthians 11:23-27*

Few of us would have the fortitude to live through what St. Paul lived through, nor are most expected to do so. But the fact remains, for too long, Catholics have been among the silent majority. Statistics would indicate they are at the table where important decisions are made. In the U.S., one in five adults identify as Catholic, and yet too often, they don't speak up, either because of the social pressures of a cancel culture or because they have a poor understanding of the social teachings that are the bedrock of their faith. They do not understand the office they received at Baptism that anointed them as prophets, "given the ability and responsibility to accept the gospel in faith and to proclaim it in word and deed" (Christifideles Laici, 25).

Plus, fear can be a powerful motivator and is the enemy of the would-be evangelist. What if I say the wrong thing? What if they laugh at me? What if they know more about the Bible than I do?

Sound familiar? Pope Francis spoke often about the importance of speaking up for the faith and also talked about the harm that fear can do.

"It weakens us, diminishes us, it even paralyzes us," he said.

There are also many Catholics who remain silent because they are influenced more by the constant bombardment of messages they're receiving from the popular culture than they are by the teachings they may have learned earlier in their faith lives, but to which they may not have returned since, or with which they simply disagree.

To be the one who stands up against that wave of public opinion requires great love and great courage, but for those who do fight through the fear, there is the consolation of knowing that evangelists don't go into battle alone.

"The Advocate, the Holy Spirit that the Father will send in my name –
he will teach you everything and remind you of all that I told you."
– John 14:26

Soldiers in God's Army

Luis Fernando Calvo lives and works in Costa Rica, a country that provides a good illustration of what is happening in much of the world where Catholics have traditionally held sway. The country claims a population that's 42% Catholic, and in fact, it is one of the few countries that still claims Catholicism as the state religion, but the number of people who identify as Evangelical is rapidly growing there. As a university teacher trained in theology, political philosophy, and more recently the social doctrine of the Church, Luis believes he knows why.

"Catholics aren't visible socially, and the society... pop culture... is moving toward a capitalistic perspective. We tend to do that where religion is concerned," he said.

When the grounding is superficial, he believes the tendency is to seek out interesting venues rather than deeply rooted faith experiences. People looking for a Sunday fix go "where the best music is played, where people greet you at the beginning of the service, where the pastor knows your wife and knows your name," he added. "The building is nice because they tend to be wealthier. That attracts people. We're moving to a different culture, and Catholicism is not well represented in it."

Luis teaches university classes on Catholic Social Doctrine and has noticed a lot of confusion among Catholics in that area.

"People think it should be an NGO, that the Church's main function is to feed the poor rather than to spread the Gospel. The Church is softening its message and trying to accommodate the culture, and that's part of the problem," he said.

He sees putting an end to abortion as one of those areas, and it's one he's passionate about. So passionate, in fact, that he began a pro-life initiative in Costa Rica, but he found it very difficult to get fellow Catholics involved, even though 80% of the programs offered were free.

What he has since come to realize, he said, is the need for better formation for Catholics, particularly those who identify more with the moral code of society at large than they do with the faith they were handed at their Baptism and Confirmation. He now believes overcoming that morality shift is a job that requires an army of lay leaders.

"Catholics need to train themselves and organize so they can better impact the culture. They are too laid back, and they don't feel the menace that's out there," he said.

Perhaps they have trouble hearing God's call amid all the noise of modern life. Hearing the call has not been Luis' problem. Separating God's voice from the noise has been his biggest challenge.

Giving Up the Silence

Luis has always loved to sit in silence with a good book. As a husband and father of three in a busy household, the silence he's craved hasn't always been easy to come by. And yet, he has looked for those moments when he could be alone in the quiet to read and to think.

Luis learned early to value his faith. The child of divorced parents, he was baptized Catholic, but religion was not a big part of his upbringing. His father was Protestant, his mother a lapsed Catholic. He discovered the Church on his own in his late teens after attending an ecumenical Christian retreat with a group of friends.

The way he explained it, "They were respectful at the retreat. They said, 'If you're Catholic, go back to your Catholic Church,' so that's what I did."

He added, "My father tried to tell me about all the errors of the Catholic Church, so I went to talk to a priest, who helped me out. It was a mysterious tool that God used to take me back to the Church."

He was a regular after that, drawn specifically to life causes.

His initial career path was a traditional one. Always attracted to education, Luis earned a master's degree in business administration and worked in the corporate world for several years while he and his wife, Alejandra, an architect, began their family. But after a few years, he felt he could no longer ignore the pull to something deeper.

After receiving his second master's in theology and political philosophy, his initial hope and plan was to launch a new political party in Costa Rica. But it turned into something different. What began as a pro-life initiative has today become a non-profit political think tank: the Tomás Moro Institute. But first, he had to leave behind the comfort and certainty of a job where salary and benefits were guaranteed.

"As with every decision, there are parts where you need to really decide if you want to go along with God's will," he said. "For me, it's been a difficult path in terms of surrendering totally to God, saying, 'I don't know if I'll be financially stable in the future, I don't know if I'll be healthy in the future, but it's okay. If it's your will, then your will be done.'"

His first task was to convince his wife that doing the work of the Holy Spirit would pay its own dividends. He said she's on board now, but he still gets pushback from family members who know he could earn more and be more financially stable working in the corporate world.

"They believe I'm wasting my precious years on causes that don't pay back as much as a corporate job," he said with a smile. "My sister will say, 'You've studied so much. Why don't you get a real job?' Maybe she wouldn't say a real job, but that's what she means. But I say to my family, 'Can you look back for a moment and say we haven't had a roof, or food, or bills paid?' We've had everything we've needed for the last 18 years. God has never failed us."

But that doesn't mean God hasn't asked much of Luis. He was willing to give his all, not knowing what would be asked of him.

"In 2021, I really said to God, 'Let's go ahead. I'm all yours. I'll be a good son. Whatever you want to send, I'll accept it,'" he said.

Two weeks later, he woke up with a high-pitched ringing in his ears, something he describes as a loud beeping noise. It was a sound he could not ignore. It lasted for several weeks until he went on retreat. It was a great relief to wake up there and realize he was again able to hear and appreciate the silence. But it didn't last. A month later, during Easter Mass, the loud ringing returned, and it's been there ever since. It's robbed him of the thing he loved—that quiet time when he could be alone in his own head, thinking, reading, and learning in silence.

"It's been a daily challenge, and a big loss for me," he said. "The first year was very hard. First, there's the medical. You try to find out what's causing it, but there are often no easy answers, and nothing can really get rid of it."

Treatment typically involves trying to drown it out to make it less noticeable—not a great solution for somebody who values silence. What made it worse, Luis said, is that those who don't suffer from tinnitus don't understand how all-consuming it can be, and how disruptive to daily living.

"The audiologist was indifferent. He told me you just have to live with it. That's one of the things that really hurt." He shrugged his shoulders, as one shrugging off a problem, then added, "Telling your friends, telling your family that you have this condition, they're..." and he shrugged again.

He agrees it's not like a condition you can see, like a broken leg or a cancer diagnosis, so people who've never experienced it aren't necessarily sympathetic. He said they don't understand things like audio sensitivity that can cause loud noises to be painful. Nor do they understand his explanation of why he sometimes has difficulty falling asleep when the rest of the house is quiet, but for him, there's a sound like a dump truck's backup alarm going off in his head. He's had to make big changes in his life, and he said it was hard in the beginning, knowing he'd probably have the condition for the rest of his life.

"At first, I prayed to get rid of it. But I think it will save me time in Purgatory, so now I thank God for it," he said. "It's taught me that suffering can have a reason, that it doesn't have to be pointless. It's part of the Christian life to take up your cross, and I thank God for that."

He has not closed the door on a political future, but for now, his focus is on the Tomás Moro Institute. The work they do is based on promoting the social doctrine of the Church, counseling women who are seeking alternatives to abortion, working with politicians on the cause of life, and helping Catholics who work in the public sphere.

"We decided the approach to take is to work with the culture that makes you think abortion is okay, to try to change that thinking," he said.

Changing a culture is a big job, but Luis has come to realize that leadership involves surrender, saying "yes" to God's will even in difficult circumstances—despite pushback, despite physical discomfort, and even when the odds seem overwhelming. It's slow going, but the Holy Fathers have always insisted there can be no compromise on any procedure that takes life or denies life. In *Humanae Vitae* in 1968, Pope Paul VI pointed out that because God is the ultimate creator, to interfere with life between conception and natural death is to usurp his ultimate authority.

"The Church is the servant of the truth," Luis said, "and we, as Catholics, participate in that truth. If we don't share that truth with the world, the world will be in darkness. We, as Catholics, have something that no one else has - the truth about God, about the human person, about society, about the reason for our existence and how we can live a fulfilled life. You cannot know that if you don't know God. It's a serious responsibility that we've been entrusted with."

Chapter Four

"Before I formed you in the womb I knew you,
Before you were born I dedicated you, a prophet to the nations
I appointed you."

~ Jeremiah 1:5

The cause of life is an area that creates great separation, even among Catholics today, and yet it is a non-negotiable according to Church teaching. The Catechism clearly states that, "Human life must be respected and protected absolutely from the moment of conception ... This teaching has not changed and remains unchangeable." (CCC 2270)

In the United States, there are Catholics in both the Democratic and Republican parties who urge compromise on the abortion issue, but that compromise in some areas would mean a change to those teachings, something that the Church, according to its own core tenets of faith, simply cannot do.

"I don't think that it's ever helpful to compromise on what is not true," said Bishop Olmsted, "because truth and love have to walk together. They won't hold up unless they do."

But, he said, that doesn't mean there is no room for the two sides to draw closer.

For example, there are some in the U.S. Congress who say if Catholics truly believe that life is a gift in every phase of development, then the laity must do much more to support women who are considering abortion or to help those women who have already had abortions to find healing, as well as help them find and pay for alternatives when faced with unplanned or unwanted pregnancies.

Clearly, society has deep divisions on the issue. But Bishop Olmsted said one thing is clear: shouting each other down doesn't and hasn't worked. He said listening is key.

"I think we always have to make an effort to keep staying with the truth," said Bishop Olmsted. "But continue to listen to see if there's someplace that we can make some compromises and work together for improving and addressing the issues at hand."

At the same time, Bishop Olmsted agrees there are some areas where the Church simply cannot back down, because he believes the core of the argument is God's intention for family life, at the heart of which is marriage.

"I don't think it would be helpful to back away from the Church's teaching on marriage," he said. "I think marriage is the basic cell of society, and I think it's moving away from the Church's teaching that really has weakened marriage. So much of our society is highly sexualized, over sexualized, and so there's a need to have real, clear teaching. I think one of the things I like about *Theology of the Body* is that Pope St. John Paul II saw clearly that the Church's teaching was right, but it didn't sound like good news, it just sounds like right news. So, we need to put it in a way that has a clear sense of the goodness of this teaching. I think we need to continually focus along that line."

Talking is one way, but modeling is another, and perhaps a more effective way. Catholic Social Teaching would indicate that the best way to further the cause of life is by treating all people as if they have the face of Christ, from the moment they are conceived until God calls them home. It's not an easy task in today's world, but it is a vital one.

In *Christifideles Laici*, John Paul II points out that our dignity is "the most precious possession of an individual. As a result, the value of one person transcends all the material world." (37) This is something Abby Sinnett learned early.

"Let all who arrive be received as Christ"
– Rule of St. Benedict, LIII

The air in the Peruvian Andes is very thin. The people who live there have adapted over the centuries, with larger lungs that help them deal with the low oxygen levels. But for outsiders, even a short-term visit can mean breathlessness and the unpleasant effects of altitude sickness. It's typically windy and cold in Ayaviri, a town with a population that hovers at around 22,000 people who are spread out over rugged, high mountain terrain. Given these detractors, it's not particularly popular with tourists, and medical missions that are typical for other parts of Central and South America are not as common in the high Andes towns. But for Abby Sinnett and her extended family, the altitude wasn't the deterrent it might have been for others.

"Many of the people who would maybe come and serve up there are from sea level, so they don't tolerate it very well," she said. "But being from Colorado and living in the mountains, we can handle the altitude."

A life of service comes naturally to Abby. Mission trips are a family endeavor, something her parents did and encouraged. She became an evangelist missionary with NET Ministries right out of high school, before getting married and enrolling in college to become a labor and delivery nurse, all while beginning a family of her own. She became interested in nursing while watching her mother, Dede Chism's, career.

"She was a labor nurse... and I got to see my first baby born with her when I was in fifth grade on Take Your Daughter to Work Day," she said. "I got exposed to healthcare really young and just loved it."

Her mother eventually went back to grad school to become a nurse practitioner, another path that Abby followed. But she said it was still those early moments with her mom that set the stage.

"When I was in high school, she brought me to another delivery, and it was at that delivery where I got to see how she was working with the doctors and the nurses and interacting with the patient, and just the beauty of that interaction and the sacredness. I always say it felt like angels were just dancing in that delivery room. It was just beautiful to see how the doctors and the nurses all just kind of interacted and were part of that couple's life in a really sacred moment. That made me want to go into nursing," explained Abby.

When the two of them joined the rest of the family on those first mission trips to Peru, it was in Ayaviri where she and her mother eventually got their first inkling that their lives were about to change forever. Her father, Ken, served as the logistician for the trips. He did much of the planning and recruiting to get others on board, making many of the arrangements, setting up schedules, and seeing to security along with her brother and later with Abby's husband, Justin, both of whom are firemen and paramedics. Their attention to those details allowed Abby and her mom to put their extensive backgrounds in obstetrics and gynecology to their best use.

The Sinnets and the Chisms make their home in Englewood, CO, which has an elevation of just under 5,400 feet heading into the Rocky Mountain foothills, but it's relatively low compared to Ayaviri, which reaches nearly 13,000 feet into the Andes. The women who live in that extreme environment are tough because they must be. The climate is

39

harsh with cold and wind, especially at night. The people battle it by dressing in layers, often in traditional sweaters and skirts.

"The women are oftentimes colorful on the outside," remembered Abby, "but it's layers and layers of skirts—like 13 skirts—and layers and layers of sweaters. When you take care of them, you have to dig through all their layers to find these little, bitty, petite bodies. And their skin is dark and kind of leathered from the elements up there, because it's very, very cold. And then the sun comes out, and it's very intense."

She explained that it's not just the environment that shows on the women's faces, though; it's what they experience just getting through the day.

"They've worked really hard all their lives, and they have many children. They'll have one on their front and then another tied to their back, and maybe they've got one on both sides," she explained. "They've got their children kind of tucked into these little blankety papooses, and they're just walking and walking to come see us. The women would walk literally five, ten, fifteen miles to come and see us at our mission site. They'd get up very early and maybe ride bikes or these little scootery things and wait for hours in the line to be seen. Our team would be about 50 people, and we would see about 1,300 people over the course of three days."

Very often, that long walk to a medical mission is their only chance to see a doctor, and their physical ailments can be very serious. Peru has one of the highest rates of cervical cancer in the world—one of the reasons Abby and her mother were drawn to the community. But often, the women's emotional scars are even worse.

"In Peru, it's just very broken, it's very poor, and there's a lot of abuse," said Abby. "The theme that the local women would tell us over and over again is, 'He doesn't love me unless he beats me,' that kind of mentality. We hear some really sad and traumatic stories of abuse, and we were able to talk to the women about their dignity and their worth and their goodness, and how they deserve to be treated well— that they don't need to be beaten, that they are good, and they are loved, and they are beautiful. It was just a rare thing for them to hear."

One night after seeing women all day and hearing their stories, Abby and her mother went to the rooftop to rest and discuss the day. They had been spending time in prayer, asking God what their next steps should be, and Abby said she felt something stirring in her heart.

"I was just feeling like He was saying there are people who are broken everywhere, and you don't have to come to Peru to find them. People are broken at home, too. It was an invitation," she said.

What grew out of that moment was Bella Health & Wellness in Englewood—a different kind of clinic that is mission-based, where patients' medical needs are seen to, but so are their spiritual needs.

"We do medicine really well," Abby said, "But what we are here for is to get souls to heaven, and the way we do that is with love. We encounter people, we enter into their stories. People say math is the universal language. I actually think that love is the universal language."

Bella Health began as an obstetrics and gynecology practice with Abby, Dede, and one other physician. But over the last 10 years, it has grown into a center for family medicine, pediatric care, functional medicine, fertility education, and wellness. There are now 26 providers in a 10,000-square-foot facility that recorded 40,000 visits in 2024, with an eye toward expansion.

From its start, Abby has felt right about the decision to start Bella, but that doesn't mean it was necessarily easy when she realized God was asking her to surrender her own plans and go with His.

"I thought I was going to grad school to work in a hospital doing high-risk obstetric care. That's what I thought I wanted to do," she explained. "And so, to walk away from our jobs and the hospital, both

Mom and I—you know, you don't get trained to open a private practice in grad school. That's not at all what you learn. You learn how to take care of patients."

Today, she is the CEO of Bella and Dede is the President of the organization, but they still stress servant leadership. There is an arched doorway in the waiting room not far from the reception desk that leads to a chapel. The day begins there with prayer in which the entire staff participates no matter where they are or what they're doing—whether in person or by Zoom before the morning huddle. Not everybody who works at Bella is Catholic, but Abbey said everybody who is hired has a mission spirit. It's part of the job description.

"We can train skills, we can send people to school, but we can't always train mission," Abby said. "Somebody needs to come in with that mission desire in their heart, because the most important thing we do here at Bella is what's right in front of us. That *person* who's right in front of us is the most important thing. I think there's always that temptation of 'I've got to see this many patients,' or 'I've got to get all these charges done,' or 'I've got to sign these labs.' But we work really, really hard for people to have the time and the space to be able to encounter that person and encounter them well. Does that mean we schedule fewer appointments in a day? Yes, it does mean that."

The appointment times are longer at Bella and there are more staff members per patient than at other facilities, because, she said, it takes more resources to be able to run a clinic with that kind of mission spirit.

"We're not just a factory on a conveyor belt of people coming in and out. Dignified, Christ-centered care is not about a machine. It's about encountering. It's about love. We meet people at a time when they are at their most vulnerable," she said.

Among the important work they do is helping couples who encounter fertility issues to become pregnant, and they work with women who wish they weren't pregnant to find life-affirming solutions at a time in their lives when they are in crisis. And as part of that, she said, they take the time to listen to patients, to pray with them, and journey with them.

"I think this is one of the loneliest times in society," she said, "and research shows the increase in anxiety and depression is continuing to rise—people just need contact. They need to be in relationship. They need to have people willing to enter in, and that's what we do. We enter into their story. We all have a battle that we're fighting, and we enter into that mess. It's not that we can fix it or solve it, but we can enter into the battle with someone. We aren't meant to do things alone. We're meant to be in communion with people."

Bella's 2024 annual report states its mission as building "a legacy that lasts an eternity, as lives are saved, people are made whole, and souls [are] getting to heaven."

Today, Abby can reconcile the work she does with the training she received because she can see the link in the chain of events that brought her from the labor and delivery room to the boardroom.

She sums it up this way: "There was a moment where I said, 'God, you called me to be a missionary, and you called me to do ministry, and yes, the skill set that you gave me to do that was through medicine.' It was letting go. It was definitely a surrender."

Chapter Five

*"Whoever wishes to come after me must deny himself,
take up his cross, and follow me."*

~ Matthew 16:24

St. Josemaria Escriva wrote that those who wish to lead must first surrender their will to the will of the Father. That can be particularly hard for today's Catholics. We value our independence, and we lean heavily on the idea that we can decide for ourselves between right and wrong. We tend to resent it when Church leaders tell us we can't do what we wish, and even among the Church hierarchy today, there are disagreements over fundamental teachings. Arguments over what constitutes marriage, the role of women in the Church, changes to the liturgy, and when to allow the Traditional Latin Mass are just some of the issues that have caused division. It's no wonder, then, that people are confused over what the fundamental, non-negotiable beliefs are, and which are ideas that are still being worked out between the Church and the Holy Spirit.

Yet there are core beliefs that have not changed since Christ sent the first disciples out to spread the good news, beliefs with deep roots that go all the way back to the Garden of Eden. Often, people who hear those details for the first time become cemented in their faith and are ready to share it. These people can become the strongest evangelists.

Being open to God can mean ending up on a path entirely different from what one expected, and it can sometimes come with considerable heartache and suffering. Yet, those who have gone down that road find they are at peace. In his book, *Furrow*, Fr. Escriva writes:

> *"As soon as you truly abandon yourself in the Lord, you will know how to be content with whatever happens. You will not lose your peace if your undertakings do not turn out the way you hoped, even if you have put everything into them and used all the means necessary. For they will have 'turned out' the way God wants them to." (860)*

Catholic saints tell us there is holiness in suffering that, when accepted, allows us to share in Christ's passion in a way that nothing else can. Bishop Olmsted said it just makes sense, then, that we can use our suffering to evangelize others, often without saying a word.

"After all, we were saved by the suffering and death of Jesus on the cross," he explained, "and He told us, unless we take up our cross each day, we cannot be His disciples. What we need are faithful disciples today. It's almost impossible at any time in history, I think, to be a faithful disciple unless you embrace the cross that's part of your particular life at any one time."

Bishop Olmsted said a person who embraces their cross while maintaining a deep faith in spite of their pain or in the face of misfortune can be very convincing when sharing that faith with others.

"They may not focus on their difficulties necessarily, but when you're aware that they bear their hardships with courage yet maintain their conviction about the deeper issues rather than focusing on their own pain, there's something that's very convicting about that," he said.

Falling Into Surrender

Angela Carroll doesn't remember the moment she fell down the stairs or anything surrounding the moments before or after it happened. But her husband, John, certainly does.

"She had gotten up to go to the bathroom, and I wondered where she was when she didn't come back. We found her on the floor. At first, we didn't realize how serious it was. It was kind of dark. But when we turned the light on, we saw the blood and called the ambulance, and they were there in like, two minutes," John recalled.

In falling, she cracked her skull in three places, creating bleeds in three different areas of her brain. She was breathing when they found her, but he remembers it was labored. He didn't find out until much later that her respirations had stopped in the ambulance on the way to the hospital.

"We were in the waiting room for quite a while, and finally I asked the lady behind the glass if there was an update. She went back and got the doctor. That's when we found out she was intubated because she had stopped breathing on her own," he said.

At 8:00 the next morning, a neurosurgeon told John she needed immediate surgery because her brain tissue was starting to swell.

"He told me she needed an emergency craniotomy. He was very frank. He said without the surgery, she was going to pass," he said.

Even with the surgery, the prognosis was not good.

"The neurosurgeon told my husband he didn't think I was going to make it," Angie remembered.

The tissues making up the right hemisphere of her brain were pushing against her skull, and they told John the only way to try and prevent further damage was to remove the bones on that side of her head. The doctor didn't know if it would work—it was possible there was too much damage already, and there were a lot of risks involved with the surgery itself—but they knew they had to try. The only thing John knew to do at that point was to pray, and others prayed with him.

"I was taking my son, Daniel, to the hospital during her surgery to sit with me and our friend in the waiting room," John recalled, "and he asked if Adoration was open as we were passing by the Cathedral. I said it was, and he said he wanted to wait in Adoration. So, I dropped him off.

And then, an hour or so later, Carley from the Cathedral found him there praying with his hand on the monstrance and brought him to the surgical waiting room. When we asked him why he was touching the monstrance, he said he wanted to hold Jesus' hand."

John said a family friend asked if she could organize a Rosary for Angie.

"I told her the more people praying for her, the better," he said.

But he was amazed at the number of people who showed up.

"I was in the front row, and when the priest asked if I would stand and give people an update on her condition, I turned around and I couldn't believe how many people were there. Half the church was full," he said.

And it wasn't just their home parish. He said he found out later there were people praying for her all over the world.

The surgery took eight long hours, and she made it through that. But when it was over, there was little relief for the family. Not at first.

"The doctor had prepared me," John said. "After the surgery on Monday, he told me it was going to get worse before it got better. He said that on Tuesday, it was going to be worse, and on Wednesday, even worse. Thursday, he said, was still going to be bad, but we should know something by then. He tells me all this right after her surgery."

47

John was left with questions that nobody wants to think about. Would his wife be the same when she woke up? Would she wake up at all?

"The neurosurgeon didn't know what was going to happen, whether she was going to be on the road to recovery or whether I was going to be planning a funeral," he said.

But then, on Tuesday morning, just hours after the doctor had tried to prepare John for the worst, he talked to him again, but this time with a different tone.

"He said after looking at her scans that there was reason to hope!" John said.

The doctor was amazed to say that the swelling in her brain, which he had expected would continue, had stopped! And the improvements continued. John was at home trying to rest on Tuesday night, just 24 hours after her surgery, when the phone rang.

"Anytime the hospital calls, you're nervous when you pick up the phone, because you don't know what the news is going to be," he remembered, "but they told me she was breathing on her own and she was fighting the tube, so they told me they pulled it out, and she asked for water. That was quite emotional because we'd had no idea what kind of function she would have, if any. And the fact that when they pulled the tube out and she asked for water told us she could think, she could speak, and she was aware of what her body needed.

"On Wednesday, a family friend stopped by, and Angie looked at her and recognized her, said her name, and that it was good to see her, she just wished it was under better circumstances, like in our backyard. She not only recognized a non-family member, she recognized the context and made a joke!"

He said there's no explanation for it other than the power of prayer.

"I think that's what it boils down to," he said. "I think she's a walking miracle."

There were still tough days ahead, though. Angie was in the ICU for a week before she became totally aware of her surroundings, and at first, she was confused about where she was and had no memory of what had happened.

"People had to fill me in," she said, "and it was difficult for a while."

But she said it could have been much worse, adding that people in her situation often have to relearn basic skills or have to live with permanent impairments.

"Amazingly enough, I didn't. It was a little difficult for me at first to do things like read or watch complicated television shows. I was really good at watching football," she added with a smile, "but other stuff, I just couldn't really process at first. But gradually, over time, everything came back and fell into place."

It was at that point that she realized God was leading her to something different.

"God gives everything to those who surrender everything."
– Pope Francis

Angie had intended to go into medicine when she first started her university studies. Her undergraduate degree is in zoology, but eventually she realized her real love was teaching. She took that science knowledge that she'd accumulated and instead worked to instill it in children at the middle and high school levels as she and her husband moved around the country for his job. One of those moves eventually brought them to Bismarck, ND, where she was hired as the Executive

Assistant for Student Development at the University of Mary, and suddenly, she felt right at home.

"I really was hoping to be able to work at U-Mary, and so when that came to be, I was really excited about it," she said.

She was excited because she loved the work, but also because it fit with another of her passions: learning more about her Catholic faith.

"I converted to Catholicism when I was 27 or 28 years old," she explained. "It had been something in my mind for many years, since I was very young. Even though my family wasn't Catholic, they had a respect for the Catholic faith. My grandmother was friends with some nuns who had a cottage a couple of doors down from her."

She said that when she was a pre-teen, she used to hide in the bathroom of her home to make the Sign of the Cross, simply because doing so felt right.

"And in the faith I was raised in, there were always questions. Things just didn't feel complete to me," she said.

But it wasn't until they made the move to Bismarck that she and her husband began discussing converting. Still in her 20s at the time, Angela had found a faith home, work that she loved, family and friends who were close, but there was still a simmering discontent in the back of her mind.

"I was told when I was 17 years old that I would never be able to have children due to a genetic endocrine condition. I had been to doctors, endocrinologists, and just knew it wasn't going to happen, and I was angry about it for a long time. It was a big sense of pain for me because I was wondering what I'd done wrong. It was just really hard," she said.

It took many years of prayer, but gradually, her pain began to heal, until she reached a state of acceptance.

"After years of struggling with it, I finally got to the point where I realized that what was truly fulfilling in my life was God and that connection I had with Him. I knew in my heart that His plan was what I truly wanted, whatever that happened to be. I came to that point one Advent during prayer, and it gave me a sense of peace. I said, 'I would love to be a mother, I would love to have a child, but if it's not your plan for me, that's okay. I accept that. My joy comes from you.' And I just stopped worrying about it," Angie remembered.

Two months later, she woke up feeling irritable and a little nauseous. She said she knew on the one hand that pregnancy wasn't possible for her. It's what she had been told, and it had never happened in all the years of her marriage, despite the fact that she had never done anything to prevent it. Yet on this particular day, she couldn't get the possibility out of her mind.

"I just didn't feel right, and I got tired of thinking about it. So, by the end of the day, I thought, I'm going to go buy a pregnancy test and a bottle of wine. If the pregnancy test is negative, I'm going to drink a glass of wine," she said.

She never opened that bottle. Her son was born when she was 41 years old. And once again, she had to put all her trust in God.

"I started having contractions in August, and Daniel wasn't due until October. At the hospital, they hooked him up to a monitor and found out that every time I had a contraction, his heart would stop. Finally, the hospitalist said, 'Okay, I'm calling it. We have to get this baby out now!' My husband, John, said all of a sudden, there was a flurry of activity, and then I was gone. Everybody was gone from the room. There was just a light shining down on a blank spot and detritus all over the floor where the bed and I had just been. He said at that moment it was like *everything* was gone in his life. But I also remember the moment they took me out, looking at the monitor and saying, 'Lord, I trust in you; I know this is going to be okay.' And sure enough," she said, smiling, "I woke up, and there was the baby, the little twerp."

51

She didn't have a chance to say the same prayer before her brain surgery, but she said that when you have a profound experience like her fall down the stairs and everything that followed it, it can't help but change you. And it wasn't *all* a blur.

"Part of what I learned the most clearly in the hospital room and just dealing with this has been giving it over to Jesus," she said. "I had one very amazing experience when I woke from the second surgery—the one where they actually put the bone flaps back in my skull after the swelling went down. I think it was before they gave me any kind of pain meds because I was in a lot of pain, and I was very scared. My family had brought in a crucifix, and I just prayed to Jesus. I said, 'Tell me how to offer this up to you.' And I immediately saw Him with the crown of thorns, and I could see everything. I could see the thorns piercing His skin and the blood dripping. I immediately felt the pain in my own head start to intensify. And I cried out, and I said, 'Lord, what do I do?' And He said, 'Accept. And do not be afraid.' And I knew in that moment I just had to accept my weakness. I had to accept my helplessness and my need and to trust Him and just surrender."

She said the moment she did that, she felt at peace, and her fear went away.

Part of that surrender has been taking a different work path. She loved the work she did at the University of Mary, but after the fall, she needed time to recover and couldn't go back to full-time at first. She came to the realization that God was pointing her in a different direction—one that she now believes was in the back of her mind even before her accident. She works part-time for her parish while she's finishing up a master's degree in Applied Catholic Theology. At the same time, she's taking on a greater leadership role in women's faith formation. She has goals and makes plans and admits that sometimes, the pace of change can be too slow for her liking, but then she reminds herself that it's not her personal desires that are important.

"I have to remember that the overall plan is not mine," she said. "It's purely up to God, so I can't get discouraged because it's not happening on my timeline. Servant leadership should be about formation and development, but most of all, it's about serving others in your leadership role—just as Jesus said He was not there to be served, but to serve," Angie said.

Chapter Six

"For this momentary light affliction is producing for us an eternal weight of glory beyond all comparison"

~ 2 Corinthians 4:17

Human beings have always suffered from hubris, and illness can certainly remind us that we aren't in control. We need to look no further than March of 2020, the year of the Covid lockdown, for proof. It was not the world's first pandemic, but it was still a shock to many that despite all the advances in science, all our modern medicines, and all our sophisticated testing, laboratories, and theories, we can still fall victim to a tiny virus that can't be stopped.

The lockdown and the pause in gatherings that it required took their toll for a time, and while statistics show that congregation numbers have largely returned to pre-pandemic levels, some former Catholic churchgoers either gave it up altogether or decided to look elsewhere. But there were also gains and important lessons learned.

Those who chose to participate, and there were many of all ages, became experts in online visiting, worshipping, and learning. There were those who discovered the Catholic Faith by watching Mass and engaging in theology study online. Plus, when the churches reopened, many returned with a greater appreciation for what they'd missed. Not only do we crave the sacraments, but we also learned how attached we are to faith sharing, and it goes deeper than coffee and donuts after services. We found out how much we missed that sense of belonging that Communion can offer. We learned that gathering around the computer for Mass isn't nearly as satisfying as finding a place in the pew.

And though few will miss those days of lockdown and forced separation, in the end, it's possible the good will have outweighed the bad. Be assured, the Holy Spirit can find us wherever we are.

"For I know well the plans I have in mind for you – oracle of the Lord – plans for your welfare and not for woe, so as to give you a future of hope." – Jeremiah 29:11

Wendy Cano found this out in a most unexpected way. A molecular biologist by training with years of education, she thought she'd spend her life coming up with ways to save the world through science. But instead, she is answering God's call by helping to form lay Catholic leaders for the new evangelization through her work with Tepeyac Leadership Initiative. Her path to God began, in many ways, with a broken heart.

Raised in Mexico City as the only child of an artist and a teacher, she has a PhD in Philosophy of Science. Wendy was studying in Spain with the intention of going into academia.

"But in the end," she said, "I understood that I'm mortal, and I saw that there are a lot of bad things in the academic world that I didn't need in my life. I saw that power corrupts the souls of people. I'd say God sent me a lot of angels to help me make wise decisions."

Still, she said she may have needed a push to make the life change that would lead to her ultimate surrender moment. As she lived and taught in Spain, she maintained a relationship that she thought would last forever, but the man in question had other ideas.

"He called me one day and told me, 'I don't want to continue in this relationship.' After 10 years! It totally broke my heart," she remembered. "The only thing I could think to do was go to the chapel and pray. I was super sad, and I asked God, 'Please give me a sign.' Ten minutes later, I get a call from one of my former students, Fabienne from Italy, who told me he was going to come visit me in Spain. I decided that was my answer, my sign. The next day, I was showing my student around—now my friend. It was healing for me. I saw that life would go on."

It was at that moment that she decided she'd give up on trying to control her own life and instead would turn it over to God. She kept up with her work and simply waited. One day, another friend, a nun named Lourdes, told her about a dream she'd had, where she described how she'd seen Wendy married with a baby. It was very detailed. They were on a beach as if on vacation. Sr. Lourdes was there, too, and they were eating ice cream.

"I told her she was crazy. My boyfriend had just left me, and besides that, Lourdes was in a cloistered community. She never left it. She couldn't leave it," she said.

And then there was the baby. Like Angela, Wendy had always known she would never be able to have children. Born with a painful immune disorder, her doctors had told her from childhood that pregnancy was not an option for her, and all her doctors into adulthood had agreed with that diagnosis. Still, Sr. Lourdes insisted.

"She told me, 'You have to trust God,'" Wendy said.

Three weeks later, Sr. Lourdes had to leave the cloister to return home to Mexico because her mother was ill. Wendy also returned to Mexico at the invitation of the government to work on a cultural project. At the same time, Fabienne, whom she'd thought was simply her friend, flew to Mexico to tell her he had fallen in love with her, and suddenly she saw him differently.

"I didn't even really know him," she said, "but I thought of how he'd been taking care of me since the first day we met."

They went to the beach, and incredibly, they happened upon Sr. Lourdes, who was there on vacation with her mother. The two of them were eating ice cream!

"She told me, 'He's the one! He was the man in my dream that God was telling me about. He's going to be your best partner.' I wasn't sure. He was different. I thought he didn't belong to my cultural environment. He's a very humble man, but he's amazing. Now I know. God's plans are better than my plans. I just had to trust," she said.

But of course, she was still trying to do things her own way. Wendy tried to go back to Spain when the cultural project was over. The first time she showed up at the airport, she found out the ticket she had purchased was fraudulent. She tried to buy another ticket and was told her credit card number had been stolen. Try as she might, her plans to leave Mexico kept getting foiled. Yet, these were just minor annoyances.

The real turning point was Covid. When the pandemic started, everything shut down, so she was forced to quarantine along with the rest of the world. In the back of her mind, she still intended to return to Spain when the world opened back up. But then her mother became ill, and that's when a light finally went on for Wendy. At last, she saw that God had other plans for her.

"What was beginning was a complete transformation of my life, but it took me some time to see it," she said.

For Wendy, the idea of unconditional trust had always been a bit frightening. She explained how, when she was just six years old and first heard the story of the Angel Gabriel's visit to the Virgin Mary, she worried because she knew she wouldn't be able to say yes to God as Mary had done.

"I remember telling God, 'I don't know how Maria did it. She said a big 'yes' to you, but I'm not able to do it. I can't handle a baby.' I was just little, but I was super afraid. Here I was, six years old, and worried that I would get pregnant and my mother and father would be mad at me. And I was just a baby myself," she said.

That fear of disappointing others had never really left her, but finally, she was ready to trust in God's plan rather than her own. While in Spain, she had spent a lot of time volunteering, so when she heard about an opportunity with Tepeyac Leadership Initiative, she decided to reach out.

"They were asking for a volunteer who speaks English," she said.

She didn't get that position right away but received a call back several months later, and in the end, was hired by the international organization as the operations manager—a job she's able to do from Mexico City after Covid caused a shift that led to rapid growth and made TLI largely internet-based.

That wasn't the only life change. She also married Fabienne, the man who started out as her friend and over time became her life partner. Sr. Lourdes had turned out to be right, not just about the marriage, but about the baby as well.

"I went to a doctor in Mexico City, and she was telling me I looked great for my age, but agreed I wasn't going to have any babies because of all these problems. She even showed me on her screen, and I was like... I'm okay, don't feel bad for me. It was what I had expected. But two weeks later, I was pregnant. So, the impossible becomes possible. The doctor was amazed. They are going to write a special chapter in a medical journal about me because it was like a very scientific challenge," she said.

Wendy has the mind of a scientist, but in that, she said, there is always room for the Divine. It took her a while to see that His plans were different from her own, but once she did see, her life has been blessed, and she has no regrets.

"Sometimes you don't even understand why things happen, but you don't need to understand, you only have to trust Him, trust in His goodness, His faithfulness. You don't have to be afraid. God will always lead you in the right direction, even when you don't see it," she said.

Those who work with Wendy say she is quietly efficient, like a finely tuned engine that keeps TLI running smoothly. Even when you don't see her, you can be sure she's busy masterminding great things in the background, even though she doesn't seek credit. She said that's just the way she likes it.

"I can observe and see how people enjoy what's happening, I love that part," she said.

Wendy said the hard part for most people in learning to trust is letting go of personal control.

"I have learned that surrender requires humility and recognizing your limitations—and most important, acknowledging God's authority—making His will your top priority. Even when things seem unclear, even if it means making sacrifices or facing challenges, when you surrender to His purpose, your life totally changes, and in my case, the result is a big mission and a little baby!"

Chapter Seven

"Forgiveness is above all a personal choice, a decision of the heart to go against natural instinct to pay back evil with evil."

~ Pope St. John Paul II

When did anger become society's default position? Perhaps it's because people feel powerless, or perhaps it's the loss of civility that can come with the immediacy and thoughtlessness of social media rants. Perhaps it began with talk radio or the 24-hour news cycle that created a need for opinion news programming to fill time. Perhaps it was texting and smartphones and society's apparent need to hear itself talk. Perhaps it was all of these things together.

Whatever it was, the result is that we seem to have lost the ability to engage with one another calmly and rationally. Instead, we draw a line in the sand and dare those with differing views to step over it. When our neighbor offends us, we don't discuss it over the garden gate; we take him to court. Political divides make negotiation almost impossible, halting progress. Insults and name-calling are standard operating procedures. Even a drive down the interstate can be dangerous. Heaven forbid if you accidentally cut someone off! Where does it end?

Pope Francis, in a Sunday audience in Rome, warned people that anger frequently harms the person who's feeling it more than the person at whom it is aimed, even when it arises from an injustice. He called it a particularly dark vice. It's one that can sneak up on people.

"It is often not unleashed against the guilty party, but against the first offender," he told the crowd. "There are people who hold back their anger at work, proving to be calm and compassionate, but once at home, they become unbearable for their spouses and children."

He pointed out that lingering wrath destroys relationships; very often, it's the relationships with those you love the most that suffer the most, even when the anger has its beginnings elsewhere.

Christ gave us the solution. As a society, we need to remember His words—and that's especially true for our leaders and for those who wish to evangelize others. Joy is essential to the Christian faith; it's what attracts others. It's hard to have joy in an angry soul.

The pain of betrayal can be hard to give up, and forgiveness doesn't always come easily, especially when the hurt begins early. It can require a great deal of surrender and help from the divine. But for Jake Kubik, it made all the difference.

"Forgive, and you will be forgiven." – Luke 6:37

There are probably only a few places in the world that seemed safer than the streets of Wilton, ND, in the late 1990s. The population at that time was fewer than 700 souls. Built on a grid of perhaps 12 blocks, with no traffic lights and only the occasional stop sign, it didn't take long to get from the houses on the north end to the all-night Cenex gas station on the south side. To strangers, it had the appearance of a movie set. It could be any town in the American heartland—fallen on challenging times, perhaps, with some boarded-up businesses along Main Street, but friendly, the kind of place where a kid could feel safe, a good place to call home. But behind closed doors, the story was far from a storybook.

For Jake Kubik and his siblings growing up in Wilton, home was often a nightmare of uncertainty where the person who was supposed to love them the most might come flying at them from out of the darkness.

"There were too many nights when my mom would come home from work late, and she'd be drunk and angry," he recalled, "and she had this plastic spoon."

His mom worked nights at a supper club 30 miles away, and he and his little brother were left in the care of their older sister. She did her best to shield them, but she was also just a kid. Jake said he and his brother would lock their bedroom door before going to bed at night so that their mother couldn't get at them when she came through the door in the wee hours, because she would often arrive angry. They never knew what might set her off. Perhaps it was a toy left out, or dishes left undone. Or perhaps they'd done nothing at all, but things simply hadn't gone well at work.

"There were beatings with the spoon, and a lot of verbal abuse, and just a lot of emotional trauma from Mom coming home drunk after work and yelling, or we'd find her in the kitchen, almost passed out, sitting at the table just blasted. It was traumatic to see," he said.

One night in particular stands out. He was ten, and his little brother was eight.

"She had that spoon, and she was pounding on the door, super mad. I remember talking to my brother, kind of game-planning on how we needed to open the door and kind of push our mom out of the way and get out of the house. We kind of rushed her. She was drunk, and she stumbled into the other room, and we ran out. It was the middle of the night," he said.

He said they ran out into the darkness, scared, but more frightened of her than of what they might encounter on the street. There they were, two little kids in their pajamas, walking alone, from one end of their small town to the other until they reached the lights of the Cenex. Jake said he remembers being frightened, but not in the way most children would be.

"It was more of an adult nervousness. A child should probably be thinking of the dangers that would be lurking in the darkness but because of the traumatic experiences we'd had up to that point, we were desensitized and more aware of the dangers that other adults could pose to us. So, nervous while we were walking, yes, particularly because it was me and my younger brother, me being the older one, and wanting to get him to where we were going. Yeah, a scary situation," he explained.

When they got to the Cenex, the cashier called their father, who lived several hours away in another town.

"He was on the road right away to get to us. But we sat in that gas station for three hours, waiting for him to show up, which he did. By then, the sheriff had also come. My dad must have called him and told him what the situation was," he said.

Jake said the sheriff wasn't surprised. He's pretty sure his dad had the sheriff's cellphone number, because trauma was a regular thing in Jake's household. His parents had been divorced since Jake was two. They had three children between them, and while there were court battles over custody and fights over her fitness to raise them, he said his mother always managed to retain custody.

"She was a fantastic manipulator; still is. She could lie through her teeth and always managed to pull out a story that would convince the judge that things were fine, and she'd take us home," he said.

Even so, he said everybody in town knew about their situation. There would be fights, the sheriff would arrive, and he'd say to the kids,

"Mom's drunk?" They'd just nod their heads. Jake realizes now that people were concerned.

"My teachers and coaches would ask questions. Looking back, I realize by the things they asked that they understood what was happening, but ours wasn't the only household where people had problems," he recalled.

He knew of other kids whose parents were drug addicts or were divorced or embattled in other ways, and he remembers thinking that the situation in his house was pretty normal—just another family with challenges. Besides, he said, theirs wasn't a daily nightmare like some kids. It was just a multi-day or several-times-a-week nightmare.

In the end, Jake said their dad rented a house for them in Wilton, had a phone installed in it, and gave them the keys. It was empty, and they were too young to live in it by themselves, but their father reasoned that at least it would give them a place to go instead of the gas station if they felt unsafe at home.

"We were ten and eight. We grew up fast," he said.

His dad had remarried and had another family to provide for, but after that night, Jake said he got a job nearby and moved his new wife and son closer to Wilton to keep a better eye on things. But other than child support, he felt that was the best he could do.

But there was a saving grace. Jake and his siblings were able to spend weekends with extended family on his grandfather's homestead ranch—happy times with aunts and uncles and cousins, learning to do chores and feel what it was like to be folded into his dad's big, close-knit family. Jake remembers those days as wholesome and wonderful, times he credits with helping to shape him and his siblings into successful adults despite their rough start in life.

"They were people to emulate. All my aunts and uncles and my dad really stressed that you work hard, and you earn things in life. And it was that side of the family's influence, I think, having regular exposure to it that saved us," he said.

Once he entered his teen years, a change in the law allowed him to decide for himself where he wanted to live, and he and his brother moved in permanently with their father. It was at that point that he finally had some peace in his life, and a whole new world opened up for him, one that finally had room for a loving God.

"My mom wasn't a regular churchgoer," he explained. "She was a Protestant. She always made sure we went to Vacation Bible School and church on Christmas and Easter, but my relationship with Jesus was a lot of fear-based praying. I knew there was a God, that there was someone we needed to take care of us beyond our situation, and there was a lot of fear-based surrender to just giving it to God because there really were no other options. I'd pray in tears, asking for God's help."

But after his move, he enrolled in a Catholic high school and received regular religious education. He was especially influenced by classes in Church history. He said he was convinced of the truth of Catholicism through his intellect, and his understanding steadily grew from there. But in the end, he said reason wasn't enough.

"I also needed faith. I had to surrender in order to draw closer to Him. Not to try to understand enough information to be convinced that Jesus is my Lord and Savior, but surrendering to His will in order to believe, and through that, to grow deeper in my understanding of who He is. And that surrender has repeated itself in my life, in my marriage, in service to others—to be good for my wife as a husband, for each of my three children, surrendering to God," he said.

He was a senior in high school when he was confirmed into the Catholic Church. But his toughest surrender was still to come.

"That surrender to Jesus gave me the courage to forgive my parents," he said.

Through prayer and reflection, he's developed a certain empathy toward his mother, and he said he now views her with mercy and sympathy for the trials she faced in her own growing-up years, and the things that made her turn to alcohol.

"She grew up on a farm in South Dakota, and her parents were strict. She was a rebellious child, and I don't think that rebellion ever fully left her. She got into alcohol fairly young. It caused a lot of strife," he explained.

Because he was able to forgive his mother, he's able to have a relationship with her now, although he admits it hasn't necessarily been easy. He recalls sitting down with her while he was still in college to talk about the trauma he'd faced. He doesn't lie to himself about what happened, and he hasn't recast his memory into something less traumatic, but he is able to love his mother despite all that's happened.

"I said, 'I forgive you, Mom.' And her response was, 'I have no idea what you're talking about. Did you ever starve? Did you ever not have clothes? You never wanted. I don't know what you're talking about,'" He shook his head and continued. "And that's where it lies to this day. But that conversation helped me. I have forgiven her, because I needed that."

He talked with his father, too. That conversation went differently.

"I forgave him for not fighting harder for us. He could have done more. He did a lot, but he probably could have pursued legal avenues, pushed a little harder. He broke down in tears, and he was apologetic. My dad's a great man, and my mom cast it off to the side, which is right on par with how I would expect her to behave. But I needed Jesus in order to forgive her, to surrender my pride and the anger that I had been harboring for years. It freed me."

Jake said he's faced many surrender moments in his life, and he can list them, but they tend to boil down to the same thing.

"It comes down to surrendering to be a good man. Asking Jesus to help me in my brokenness. It happens on a daily basis. I'm a broken individual who cannot be made whole without Jesus," he said.

And though he admits to his brokenness, he feels the trauma in his early life served an important purpose, one he said he didn't understand until he joined the Catholic faith.

"We view our suffering as having a purpose, and we can actually use it for the benefit of others. And I think about the resilience that it imbued me with. It has created a pragmatic nature in me that allows me not to necessarily react to other people's emotions, to have a thicker skin when it comes to business, to go my own way. It's fueled my ability to take risks," he explained.

Perhaps it was that quality that allowed him to take a leap of faith in his work life. After starting out on a traditional business path after college, he said he and his wife had determined they were on a 10-year plan. That's how long he expected to be doing the job he had. Except, it was sucking up all of his energy. He was working long hours, and it was taking him away from home too much—a real problem for a man with a young family. He said he had taken the types of tests that young professionals take to determine his gifts, and one area that came up as a real strength for him was fundraising—something that seemed to fit with his personality as a thick-skinned risk taker.

"It was my wife who found, unprompted by me, this 'major gifts officer' position. At the time, we were living in Rapid City, SD. We'd just finished building a house. A move wasn't in our 10-year plan, but God takes care of us in His own timeline," he said.

He interviewed for the job and got it, and in the dead of winter, during a snowstorm, they made the move.

"It's been a blessing ever since," he said. "Not without challenge, but God has a greater plan that's always better than ours, and we just have to ride it out long enough to see how His love is enacted in our lives."

From that first job, he moved on to major gift fundraising at a university before starting his own business, teaching non-profits how to go about generating major gifts on their own. That was truly a risk, but he felt drawn to it by the Holy Spirit, and he said he finds great satisfaction working in the non-profit arena. He said the conversational style when it comes to fundraising is not too different, but the work is better when it's motivated by leaders with servant hearts.

"When you're working for a non-profit and you truly use the money you bring in to cycle back into the mission, I just think the mechanism of the non-profit and how they utilize the money from a governmental and tax perspective provides a mindset of servant leadership that is superior to that of a for-profit counterpart, and that's really been a draw for me. I find these people so mission-focused... there's just a different mindset that comes along with nonprofit work," said Jake.

Jake knows that for most people and organizations, fundraising is among the biggest challenges they face. But he teaches that success requires more than asking for money, it also requires action in spreading Christ's message while building and maintaining relationships, something he learned to do by letting go of anger, forgiving those who hurt him, and allowing himself to feel the love that surrounds him, a love that he gives back in joy to others.

"Those forgiveness conversations were breakthroughs for me in my relationship with my parents," Jake said. "Only Jesus allowed those conversations to happen and to give me courage to do that. Which, really, one could argue is a form of surrender in itself, because you have to surrender bitterness and anger in order to forgive, right?"

Chapter Eight

"I give you a new commandment:
love one another as I have loved you"

~ John 13:34

There's a common saying in corporate leadership circles: leaders are made, not born. There is some truth to that. Consider St. Peter. When the chips were down, he denied the Son of God not once, but three times, yet in the end, he led the founding of a faith family that would change the world. What Peter needed was the strength he received from the Holy Spirit at Pentecost—a gift every confirmed Catholic has also received. In other words, the foundation is there for all of us to be the kinds of leaders the Apostles were, the kind of leaders who are world changing. What is needed now is Catholics with the courage to take on the challenge first laid down by Christ, to go out and spread the Good News.

In *Apostolicam Actuositatem*, the Second Vatican Council wrote that the laity have not only the right, but the duty to be missionaries of the faith, adding that it was necessary "to intensify the apostolic activity of the people of God," calling our role "indispensable." (1)

We are still far from the ideal of evangelizing the entire world, but the idea of creating leaders who are not afraid to speak their truth in secular circles is a giant step, and the deepest impression they can make is in their firm commitment to their own moral character and their care and compassion for others. St. Thomas Aquinas said leadership is about serving others, particularly the most vulnerable, and placing the good of others before one's own. In this way, all work can be a form of prayer when done in accordance with God's will.

Sometimes those we are looking to save are just a heartbeat away.

"Entrust your works to the Lord, and your plans will succeed."
– Proverbs 16:3

You really never know how a promise may impact your life. Andres Martin was just 14 years old when, in a moment of desperation, he promised God he would do whatever was asked of him. As it turned out, what was asked involved saving someone else.

His story begins, as so many stories do, with heartbreak.

"My father left us," he explained, abandoning him, his mother, and his five siblings to fend for themselves.

But there were better times ahead.

"My mother sought an annulment and remarried an outstanding man who took on six kids. He'd never had children before, and he took on a whole family," he explained.

So, for a while, at least, there was stability.

Like most boys, Andres had a love for adventure, and as the middle child in a family of five boys and one girl, he said he always loved a challenge.

"I was a big 'Mission Impossible' fan, and the second movie had just come out," he explained. "There is a scene in the beginning where Tom Cruise is climbing a mountain, and it's a very cool scene. We had moved to Arizona, and I was fascinated by mountains. There was a mountain within walking distance from our house. And I thought he looked cool doing it, so I thought I'd probably look cool doing it. So, I took my youngest brother, Matthew, with me. He was nine at the time. I saw a path that looked like the most challenging part and decided to climb that. I told my brother to stay behind; I didn't want him climbing up."

As Andres describes it, things went well until he got near the very top. There had been construction going on in the area at the time, and the path he chose was unstable. He put his foot on a rock and realized it was about to shift out from under him. He couldn't go backward or forward. He was stuck.

"I'm probably like 50 feet up in the air, and I call down to Matt. There was another path that led to the top from the other side, and I told him to run around and grab me because I didn't think I was going to be able to pull myself up. At this point, I was very frightened. I thought to myself, I could easily fall down this mountain and die or become paralyzed. I also didn't think my little brother, who wasn't very big at the time, was going to be able to pull me up, or, heaven forbid, he could also fall while trying. I thought it was possible we could both fall. So, I did what most people do in a moment of desperation. I began to pray," he remembered.

Andres said God had always been a part of his life, growing up as he did in a Catholic family, so prayer came naturally to him, but this was truly from the heart.

"I said, 'God, please get me off this mountain, and if you do, I'll do whatever you ask of me.' I think it was nothing short of a miracle. My brother came, and with what little strength he had, he pulled me up, and the rock under my foot didn't slip out. I put that promise in the back of my mind, but it was always there," he said.

Fast forward more than a decade, and life changed for the family again. The man they had all depended on died tragically by suicide, and it sent them all into a tailspin.

"It was a dark time. It affected our family greatly, to the point that pretty much all my siblings turned to alcohol and drugs in different degrees," he recalled.

He said his little brother Matthew tried to dull the pain with prescription painkillers.

"It had gotten to the point where he was unrecognizable," he said. "I didn't want to have a relationship with him."

But God had a different idea.

"God just revealed Himself to me, and I knew that I had to do something. I started doing research on where he could go and how to get him there, and to have a rebuttal for any excuse he might make. I also decided not to tell anyone else what I was planning. I didn't want anybody trying to talk me out of it. Matt and I hadn't talked for months. It might even have been years. But I called him out of the blue and said I'd like to take him out for coffee. And that's when I presented this opportunity to him. I tied it back to my daughter. I asked him who he wanted to be for her, who he wanted to be for his future children, and who he wanted for his future self. I talked a lot about God. Prior to meeting him, I'd prayed four or five Rosaries—that day in particular, I'd prayed the most Rosaries I ever had. Thanks be to God, he said yes to treatment, and I drove him there that day," he said.

It wasn't easy. He said he knew it had to be abrupt because others in the family had been enabling Matt out of a mistaken love. Even Andres himself felt the devil's attack in pivotal moments.

"It came out pretty clearly. I felt sorry for my brother. Questions came into my head like, 'How's he going to do out there? He'll be all alone. How's he going to feel? It's cold out there. He's going to be cold, and he's not going to know anyone.' Thank God I didn't utter any of these things to Matt or slow down, because that was a turning point in my brother's life," he said.

Andres has made a habit of listening to God's voice, and he believes the Holy Spirit may be leading him toward a leadership role in other areas of his life as well. He is still a young man with a young family, and as the father of eight, he has a great deal of responsibility. But now he wonders if he's being prepared to answer God's call in a new way.

"After my second daughter was born, this prayer just came out of nowhere, but it came straight from the heart. I said, 'God, I know you're calling me to something. Please show me what it is. I'm open to it.' I continued that prayer for about four years. And by happenstance, I met with a business owner, and we struck up a conversation about God in general. He didn't know I was Catholic. And he says to me, 'You know, I have a friend who's starting a program that I think you'd be really good for,'" he explained.

The acquaintance suggested he check out a website, which happened to be for Tepeyac Leadership Initiative. A few days later, Andres received a call from TLI Executive Director Cristofer Pereyra, who told him that the business leader—a mutual friend—had mentioned his name.

"I told him I was too busy to take on anything else, but he asked if I'd be willing to go out to lunch. Everything he said to me was the answer to my earlier prayer. He was talking about leadership, about spiritual formation and growth. He was appealing to a political side of things that I had felt drawn to," he said.

Today, Andres works in government roles, serving as an ombudsman for Maricopa County, AZ, where he solves problems between departments before they escalate into bigger issues, and as a deputy chief of staff, he works closely with the legislature. He sees the potential for a bigger role in that area in the future, but he is humble about his prospects. He acknowledges that his future may lead to political office, but he gives the credit to God and to TLI.

"I see how God has used that experience and the growth that has come from that and the opportunities as a result of being in the program, and that He is calling me to leadership in that particular sphere," Andres said.

He said he's not in a big hurry to get there, but he agrees that the time is right for servant leaders to step forward.

"I would call it transformational leadership— the type of leadership that moves people and organizations forward, but not forward in the sense that they're just meeting numbers and financial goals. They're moving in a way that helps the organization thrive. They're creating healthy cultures where people want to come to work," he said.

He explained that among the leadership concepts brought forward by TLI, in addition to the cardinal virtues of prudence, temperance, fortitude, and justice, are humility and magnanimity.

"The humility I'm talking about is really knowledge of oneself, where you don't speak highly of yourself, but you know and understand where God has given you gifts. It's not arrogant, it's just a fact," he said.

Good leaders, he explained, understand their strengths and build on them. As for magnanimity, he said the best leaders are not afraid to let others outshine them.

"Becoming great by bringing out the greatness in others—that's how you define true magnanimity. And if you don't get credit or if someone who you help ends up becoming your boss in the future, you know what? That's okay. You did your job," he said.

Looking back at that frightened 14-year-old, Andres still credits the moment when he made a promise to God as the jumpstart to a life of faith. He's not sure where it will take him, but he is taking the steps as they come and said he's open to whatever God has in store.

"I can't be more grateful to God, and I know without a doubt, whether it's because of that promise or not, that I've been truly blessed. God wants us to fully commit to Him. And I try to do that and show that through action. Because we can't be all talk, right? God calls us to do our part," he said.

As an epilogue to Andres' story, his brother, Matthew, is doing well and is also a graduate of TLI.

Chapter Nine

*"The righteous cry out, the Lord hears
and he rescues them from all their afflictions."*

~ Psalm 34:18

It's one thing to trust in God and follow his will when things are going well. When things fall apart, it gets a lot harder. As with Job, the question of "why me?" can be crushing, and the natural response can be to shut everyone and everything out and simply close up shop. That's when leaders need to double down in their witness.

One of the obstacles evangelists face today is the fallout from the sexual and financial scandals that happened within the Church in the early part of this century. There's no way to explain them away or excuse them. One can only say that all people are sinners and the sins that were committed were permitted by God because He allows free will, but that they were an attack by the evil one—admittedly an effective one—but they were not of the Holy Spirit or His Church.

Jesus promised when He gave the keys of the kingdom to St. Peter that the gates of hell would not prevail against it, and as faithful believers, we go forth in faith knowing that to be true. The Church has taken steps to overcome the sins of the past and is doing what it can to heal individuals who were hurt. Now, it looks to its lay evangelists to help with the mission of bringing people into or back to the Church, just as early followers of St. Paul helped the early Christians overcome their fear of his past persecution to hear his message. If we believe in Christ, then we must believe He can heal all wounds.

Among those helping to change minds and hearts are committed Catholic authors and journalists who are doing the hard work of reporting the truth, even when it's painful, and telling the stories that bring hope and inspiration to today's Catholics. It's a form of evangelism that has its own share of pitfalls, not the least of which can be financial insecurity and the need for thick skin. Journalists are often targets of criticism, and that can be especially true for those who take on pro-life issues. Freelancers often don't have the security of large corporations backing them up, but they go forward knowing they have Christ on their side.

"But this I will call to mind; therefore I will hope:
The Lord's acts of mercy are not exhausted,
his compassion is not spent" – Lamentations 3:21-22

Patti Armstrong has told so many people's stories in her years as a Catholic author and talk show host. Some of those stories are sad, some are miraculous, but her signature style is to bring hope to the reader or listener. Joy is her default mode. But she said nothing can really prepare you for the moment when your world comes crashing down. Her husband, Mark, died without warning when her attention was on something else.

"I was writing that morning," she said, "working hard to get an article done after I had interviewed Fr. Ehli on the phone. Mark was starting to talk with me about something, but I was too busy to really listen. He was going upstairs to take a nap, so we agreed we would talk later."

It's not as if the two of them hadn't spent time together that day. They'd ridden their bikes to morning Mass and, in the early hours, he'd gone cross-country skiing while it was still dark. He'd been awed by his views of the Northern Lights and had even posted the photos to Facebook. When he sent them to their parish priest, Fr. Joshua Ehli, asking him what they reminded him of, the answer was immediate. They were just like the rays from the heart of Jesus, the ones made famous in the Divine Mercy picture. It was a good day until it wasn't.

When Mark came downstairs, he lay on the couch and seemed agitated. Patti knew there was something wrong. He said he was having severe pain in his chest. His younger brother had died of a sudden massive heart attack, so Patti wasn't taking any chances. She didn't wait for paramedics, but instead, got him into the car and to the nearby hospital emergency department within minutes.

"The pain was caused by an ascending aortic tear, and he needed immediate surgery," she recalled. "Three of my 10 children had joined me at the hospital right away, with two more on their way. It would be a four-hour wait before surgery. Suddenly, I felt as if someone next to me was telling me: 'Get him Last Rites!'

"'Oh yeah,' I thought. You can ask for that before major surgery. I expected him to survive the surgery, but thought it would be a good idea regardless, so I called Fr. Ehli again. He had gone to a funeral after our earlier interview. He told me he'd just returned to Bismarck. He said, 'I'm in my car, which hospital are you at?' He was there in less than 10 minutes."

Patti and five of their 10 children were there to pray with him before he headed into the operating room. Mark was ready to see to his own soul, but characteristically, his first concern was for her.

"Here he was, having this terrible pain, and he kept asking our daughter if I was alright," Patti said.

A year earlier, to celebrate Mark's retirement, they had gone on a pilgrimage to Spain and Portugal to be in Fatima on May 13, the Feast of Fatima and Mark's birthday. While overseas, Patti developed severe abdominal pain and ended up hospitalized for five days with diverticulitis that showed signs of turning into an overwhelming infection. She spent most of her time in Europe with increasing pain. All she could really do was offer it up, and she was grateful when she was finally well enough to continue the trip in a scaled-back capacity. Mark was going to Adoration and visiting churches, and he shared with Patti that he had asked God to give him the suffering instead of her.

When she heard this, she appreciated his love and concern, but said she told him, "No, this is for me. How would I even get around without you being in charge, since you speak Spanish and I don't?"

She said it was a blessed time, despite the pain she was in.

Upon returning home, there were periodic flare-ups, but she hoped she could manage them by controlling her diet. During the previous year, Patti had been traveling to Michigan frequently to help care for her elderly father, who was turning 99 years old. Mark knew she had a lot going on, and he'd been praying for her.

Patti and Mark hadn't always been strong in their Catholic faith, but they had always wanted to make a difference by doing good in the world. They met in the Marshall Islands while serving in the Peace Corps. Patti will tell you that she didn't like him very much at first. He had a strong personality, so did she, and they tended to argue more than connect. That particular trait would remain with them throughout their time together, but slowly, they discovered a kinship in the things that truly mattered and a bond that she said grew to be unbreakable. Their lives over the years became so entwined that they were in almost constant communication about everything they did, whether they were together in the same room or halfway across the country from one another.

She readily admitted they were both poorly catechized when they met, although they had Catholicism as a basic foundation from which to start. They didn't necessarily follow Church teachings to the letter when they were young and newly married.

"Over time, though, we began to attend Mass every Sunday, not just when we felt like it," she said. "We became inspired by good books. We were reacquainted with Our Lady of Fatima, learned about Our Lady of Guadalupe, and started praying the Rosary. Together, this set into motion a deepening of our Catholic faith, although it took years and there were bumps along the way."

As with many Catholics, Patti said they tended to pick and choose which tenets of the faith to follow and which to decide for themselves. They were married and the parents of two boys when they decided their family was complete, but they later changed their minds and decided to let God in on the decision regarding family size. They went on to have eight more children, six boys and two girls. The couple also adopted two boys from Kenya, East Africa. Life in their busy household was chaotic, but they always made room for prayer.

"Raising 10 children and being in a marriage with two strong personalities meant that peace and harmony sometimes eluded us. But we began surrendering, beginning with Mark becoming unemployed from a small radio station in Montana when we were expecting our fourth child," Patti said. "We surrendered to God, accepting our situation, asking only to find a good place to raise a family and grow in holiness."

A month before Mark's unemployment compensation ran out, she said he received a job offer from a radio station in Bismarck, ND. He had not even applied for the job but received the offer through word-of-mouth when the station manager was looking for a reporter in the radio newsroom.

"Thirty-five years later, it's clear that God answered our prayer. When we moved to Bismarck in 1990, it had many active Catholic parishes, but it has really blossomed. More people attend daily Mass in the Diocese of Bismarck than anywhere else in the country. Such Mass attendance has surely contributed to thriving vocations, many hours of Eucharistic Adoration, long lines for the sacrament of reconciliation, and so much more to the lively faith of our community," she said.

That faith community would be very important in the days and weeks ahead. Mark's surgeon worked for hours to try to repair the damage to his heart, but the tissues weren't strong enough to hold, and they couldn't save him. Patti said that at first, she was simply in shock.

"Initially, I didn't know how I could go on without him. How would I find meaning again in anything, since he had been so involved in all aspects of my life?" she remembered.

She said she was immersed in the pain of loss, but her grief was eased somewhat by her children, her faith family, and the community that had known them both so well. And she also felt some gratitude.

"I accepted God's plan because it was already something I had determined many years ago—surrender to God, whatever happens. I found things to thank Him for, such as Mark getting Last Rites, the fact that our youngest had just finished college, the fact that Mark's brother died 15 years earlier, so perhaps God gave him some bonus years while we were still raising our children," she said. "Slowly, the light and love of my husband began coming through so that through the dark clouds, shimmers of life began to flicker. It's been gradual, but I know that I am blessed by the love of family and friends. So many times, I feel God's care through them."

Seven months after Mark died, Patti's diverticulitis worsened to the point where her life was at risk. She needed major surgery to remove a large section of her colon. Her doctor told her he was shocked at the extent of the damage. A surgery that typically would have taken three to five hours took seven, and she needed a temporary ileostomy pouch on the outside of her stomach to allow her colon to recover. That meant another major surgery six weeks later to reverse it. As a result of the urgency for surgery, she was unable to visit her father when she knew the end was coming, nor could she be with her five siblings at his funeral.

"But through it all," she said, "I felt God's grace holding me up and giving me the strength to accept everything and offer it up as a sacrifice, united with the suffering of Jesus like a prayer. And now, rather than praying together every evening for our children, I trust that Mark is continuing those prayers with me in eternity, hopefully in heaven, but as a Catholic, I know to keep praying for him, too."

"Keep repeating them to your children. Recite them when you are at home and when you are away, when you lie down and when you get up." – Deuteronomy 6:7

Patti and Mark both felt that their primary leadership responsibility was and still is to evangelize their children. As the parents of 10, and now with 21 grandchildren, it's always been a big task, and it's required a lot of prayers. For 19 years, they homeschooled their kids through middle school, then made the financial commitment to send them to Catholic high school. And although all of them graduated strong in their Catholic faith, Patti said not all have gone the distance, at least not so far.

She said, "At times, Mark and I wondered, 'What could we have done differently? What do we need to do to get our children back to God?'"

She and her friend and fellow writer, Roxane Salonen, co-wrote a book on parenting called *What Would Monica Do?* It talks about this very subject, offering advice to worried parents of fallen-away children. Patti said it wasn't a book she initially wanted to write.

"I said no. I already planned to write a book, but I was waiting for everyone to come back to the faith so that I could write about 10 happy endings. In all honesty, that would have been a terrible book, as if I would be able to impart a blueprint to get prodigals back into the fold. Life isn't that easy. There are no specific instructions to follow, a number of prayers or sacrifices to be made that will fix everything. We can seem to do the same things as someone else and not necessarily get the same results," she explained.

Roxane convinced Patti to write the book that she wished she'd been able to find, one that would accompany other parents on the same path, under the example of St. Monica.

"Since we were both in the Catholic media, it meant being public about the fact that some of our children have left the faith. We know other Catholics in the media in the same situation who choose to keep that information private," she added.

She said it can be humiliating to devote one's life to working in and for the Church, only to end up with children who have walked away. It invites judgment from people whose children did not stray or whose families are still young.

"To be honest," she said, "back in the day when all of our children were enthusiastically Catholic, I would have judged someone like me as in some way failing to do a good enough job."

With all that in mind, she finally agreed to write the book with Roxane.

"The message which we've taken to heart is that we can fill ourselves up with inspiration and hope, but in the end, going deeper in our own faith is the best thing we can do for our children, all while surrendering them to God," she said.

She takes the same approach when it comes to the work she's doing to help draw others to Christ. At first, Patti couldn't imagine going back to work and finishing up all the assignments and deadlines she had looming, but she still had financial obligations to meet, and she also still felt a pull to draw others to God. She said that like all people, there are always things she wishes she'd done differently, things she can't change. She still wishes she'd taken more time with Mark on that last morning of his life. But in an interview on her son Luke's social media, she admitted that it helped when he pointed out to her that regrets are for the living. She consoles herself with the knowledge that those moments don't matter to Mark now, not where he is. She said eternity feels like it's just around the corner for us all, and so she's making her priorities God and salvation.

"To surrender to God is to wave a white flag and let go of everything," she said. "It's hard. But it's harder not to do it. Why swim upstream every day when you can ride in God's lifeboat? It's not a safe haven against all storms, but instead of fighting things we have no control over, we let God lift us up and keep us afloat."

Chapter Ten

"I begin this letter with a clarion call and clear charge to you, my sons and brothers in Christ: Men, do not hesitate to engage in the battle that is raging around you, the battle that is wounding our children and families, the battle that is distorting the dignity of both women and men. This battle is often hidden, but the battle is real. It is primarily spiritual, but it is progressively killing the remaining Christian ethos in our society and culture, and even in our own homes."

~ Into the Breach

Thus begins the book *Into the Breach* by Most Reverend Thomas J. Olmsted, Bishop Emeritus of Phoenix. When he wrote this letter and the book that followed, Bishop Olmsted didn't realize the spark it would create. In fact, he said he had no idea what would happen. At the time, Pope John Paul II had written about the feminine genius in his letter to women in 1995, and the bishop said people were asking him why the pope hadn't written something similar about men.

"So, it seemed to me people were longing for something like that, and also, I just had a sense that we needed to talk about the identity and mission of men, focusing precisely on them. So that's how it came about," he said.

Before he began writing, the bishop called together a group that included women, but also men whom he thought had the potential to be particularly influential. He asked them to arrive ready to talk about the identity and mission of men today.

"There was a deacon who was also a former general in the army. There was a coach who was very well known for getting fired because he prayed with a football team in the middle of the field at the end of a game. I chose people who were really living their faith. I felt they would be a big help to me to understand," he said.

Out of that came the Apostolic exhortation *Into the Breach*. It did well, but it really picked up traction when it was embraced by the national Catholic men's fraternal organization, Knights of Columbus. The Knights produced a video series based on the book, and many councils showed it over successive nights. Ask a member of the organization if it made a difference, and his face will likely light up.

"Oh yeah, a big difference," said Grand Knight John Berger, Knights of Columbus Council 6540. "It was basically a call to men that says, 'Hey! Wake up! The world is going to hell, and it's your fault! You guys need to start living your role. You need to be the spiritual leaders of your families!'"

Bringing his exhortation into a group setting fit right into the message of communion outlined by Pope St. John Paul II in his document *Cristifideles Laici,* in which he encourages the formation of lay groups. He points out that true change of culture can happen when a group of believers is impacted, and that impact spreads to an ever-larger circle. Plus, Christians are meant to gather and share their faith and values with one another—something that becomes increasingly important in a world that has grown indifferent, if not hostile to the tenets of the Catholic Faith. Members of a faith community journey together and can encourage one another.

"Thus I have searched among them for someone who would build a wall or stand in the breach before me" – Ezekiel 22:30

John Berger has always been a leader, taking on numerous management roles in his job as an electrical engineer at an oil refinery in the heart of America's largest oil reserves. His career trajectory has been different from most, mainly because he's been content to remain where he is. He's put roots down in his hometown and has refused to move, even if it's meant turning down promotions. But he's been promoted anyway. Perhaps the reason he's been so successful has been his take on leadership.

"Who you are being is so much more important than what you are doing," he said. "How do you define who the leaders are in any organization? One, you can get the organizational chart, and two, you can talk to people. The people will tell you who the leaders are, and it might not be the people on that organizational chart."

He went on to explain that in his experience, the natural leaders are those who people actually want to follow, because they possess the qualities of magnanimity and humility—the very qualities that mark them out as people of virtue—those people are worth following. He learned that lesson early in his career, and he's brought it with him into his faith life as well.

"When you talk about servant leadership, well, who are you serving?" he asked. "We're serving Jesus Christ. We're serving our people, but I think that leadership ultimately is built on a strong identity as a child of God. If you're a strong disciple of Christ, that's attractive, Jesus is attractive, and people want to follow that."

About five years ago, his parish priest recognized his leadership abilities and asked him to take on the role of Grand Knight within the Knights of Columbus council in his own parish in order to save it from extinction.

"The members told Father at the time that they were going to shut our council down. They said they no longer had men interested in coming to the meetings, and they really couldn't conduct business any longer. Those who were involved were burned out, and they were just ready to be done. Father asked me to get involved, and I told him the same thing. I was a Knight, but I didn't even go to the meetings either. He said, 'I think you're a leader.' Thankfully, he knew another guy who had just moved to town who was also a Knight who knew how things worked, and Father knew that I knew a lot of people in the parish," John said.

Together, they decided that if they were going to get involved, things would need to change.

"We said, 'If we're going to really grow the Knights, what does it need to be based on?'" He said it brought to mind a moment years earlier when his son came home from high school. "He asked me, 'Dad, why aren't you a Knight?' And I was like, 'I don't know, am I supposed to be?' He said, 'Father told us that we're all supposed to be Knights as we graduate high school, as men.' The boys were part of a group called Knights of Virtue in school. The priest told them they needed to continue with it, and as adults, that meant Knights of Columbus. Anyway, I was like, 'Well, I guess if my son told me I should do it, I'd better do it.' So, I joined. Of course, I could make a million excuses for why I didn't really get involved at the time. But it was a blessing when Father asked me to be the Grand Knight."

It was a blessing because that's when he became truly active. Since that time, the council has grown by nearly 100 men, most of them young and very involved, and John said a big part of that was Bishop Olmsted's book, and subsequently the video and the follow-up series made after *Into the Breach*.

"It's all based on good programming. It's not based on pancakes or any of that stuff," said John. "It's got to be based on helping men live their vocation in life with other men who are striving to do the same thing—to be good, faith-filled men. The Knights are supposed to be the strong right arm of the Church, and that's what we've been striving to do."

It didn't stop there for John. After becoming more active in the Knights, he decided he should serve the community more, so he joined the St. Vincent DePaul Society to help those in need. From there, he thought it would be important to support the Church's religious, so he joined the Serra Club as a way to pray for and encourage vocations.

"None of that was part of my plan, but I guess it was God's plan that I would find myself there. I'm a better Serran because I'm a Knight, and I'm a better Knight because I'm a Vincentian," he said.

He also credits Bishop Olmsted with inspiring him to start a men's prayer group.

"We've been meeting every Wednesday night for years, and we pray the Rosary for our children, our grandchildren, and our godchildren; we have a moment of silence, and we offer our prayer intentions. Those men who show up for that are my best friends in life. It's just 30 minutes, but the strength that comes from all those men, not just for me, for all of us, it's amazing. I look forward to that every week," he said.

Bishop Olmsted acknowledges the importance of groups like the one John described to help people grow in holiness in a society that may have been based on Christendom at one time, but which is now increasingly, if not wholly, secular.

"I don't think we've had Christendom for a long time," the Bishop reflected. "But it seems to me it's one by one that people's hearts are changed, and those kinds of changes are probably more lasting... through witness one by one, and then in family life and in smaller groups, impacting society. I think one of the groups really impacting society on a larger basis would be the Knights of Columbus because they're clearly Catholic. They have regular formation for their members at the beginning and then ongoing. So, there are some groups that are doing some really good things. That's also one of the reasons that we have the Tepeyac

Leadership Initiative and the Hour of the Laity—to try on a wider basis to influence one another in living our faith."

"For where two or three are gathered together in my name, there am I in the midst of them." – Matthew 18:20

After five years, John is ready to pass on the reins of Grand Knight.

"I just think it's time for me to step aside," he said, "because I think that's part of leadership, too—knowing when you have to let other people get involved. I'm not stepping back from it; I'm just shifting into a different role."

He said he is not burned out and points to a popular phrase used by motivational speakers: How can you be burned out if you've never really been on fire?

"That's something I think of often," he said. "Being tired is good. Work is a blessing. But being tired is not burnout. If we're on fire with the Holy Spirit, our flame will never burn out—so if we feel burned out, we should ask ourselves why. Perhaps the Lord is telling us something."

Chapter Eleven

"To be holy isn't easy, but it isn't difficult either. To be holy is to be a good Christian, to resemble Christ. The more closely a person resembles Christ, the more Christian he is, the more he belongs to Christ, the holier he is."

~ Josemaria Escriva, The Forge, #10

Holiness is the primary purpose behind the Church, and that doesn't apply simply to the ordained, but to everybody. In writing *Lumen Gentium* in 1964, the Second Vatican Council strove to dispel the idea that holiness was primarily meant to be lived out by priests and nuns, but rather, was the mission of the common priesthood of the baptized: "This is the will of God, your sanctification." (1 Thes 4:3)

Part of striving for sainthood is following the directives given to us by Christ in The Great Commission, to go out and make disciples of all nations! The title *Lumen Gentium* means we are to be a light to all nations, reflecting the light of Christ to all. When it comes to holiness, great accomplishments aren't required. Small acts accomplished with great love can do the trick. The key is the attitude with which they are carried out.

The early Christians attracted others to their movement through their love and charity toward all, an attitude that couldn't help but be attractive. It wasn't what they said, it was often what they did and how they did it. That same method of evangelization works well today.

Among the most divisive societal issues facing us today is immigration. In January of 2025, the United States Conference of Catholic Bishops outlined what it called the *Catholic Elements of Immigration Reform*. It reiterated what has been said by the Conference before—that immigration laws are overly complex and unjust. The focus, the bishops pointed out, should be on finding legal pathways to overcome decades-long wait times for those who are in the U.S., who may have entered illegally in search of a better life, but who are working. A third of them came here as children with their parents and now have families of their own. The bishops reiterate that half of U.S. farm workers in this country are undocumented. It also outlined what Catholic social teaching considers to be a basic human right, stating, "When the conditions for a dignified life are absent, people have the natural right to migrate, and countries have a duty to accommodate that right to the extent possible." (USCCB, "Catholic Elements of Immigration Reform," 6)

What should happen in theory is one thing, but what happens in reality is something very different. The issues are complex and multifaceted, and there can be no doubt that immigration is one of those issues that can make tempers flare.

"It's very politicized, and there are a lot of strong feelings about it," said Bishop Olmsted, "which makes it harder to hear one another. But we're a nation of immigrants. We've never had a comprehensive immigration program for the United States. In order for us to get that kind of political agreement together, we really need to work across the aisle with both Republicans and Democrats. But I think we Catholics have an important role to play, because Catholics are both Democrats and Republicans. So that's why I strongly encourage our people to get engaged in the culture, but also in political debate."

It's one thing to see immigration as an issue, but something else altogether when you see it by looking into the face of a person who's impacted directly. Perhaps the best argument one can make as a Catholic is to point to Mary and Joseph, who escaped Herod by fleeing to Egypt with the Son of God under their protection, entering a country where, surely, they were undocumented.

"For the Lord, your God, is the God of gods, the Lord of lords, the great God, mighty and awesome, who has no favorites, accepts no bribes, who executes justice for the orphan and the widow, and loves the resident alien, giving them food and clothing." – Deuteronomy 10:17-18

In 2008, Cristofer Pereyra was flying high. He was living the American dream. A young, newly naturalized American citizen, Cristofer had worked his way into a reporter job in a major television market. With the recognition he'd gained with his on-air work, along with his talent for business and the trust he'd earned in his community, he had also built up a successful real estate company that paid him well. He had found the love of his life, a beautiful young mother from Mexico with two equally beautiful children, a boy and a girl. He believed he had everything he could possibly want or need: a great job, a great family, a big house, a perfect life. And then, in a single afternoon, it all began to unravel. Looking back, he sees the path his life has taken as a blessing, but it would require a profound surrender before he finally found the vocation he was born to pursue.

"In all your ways be mindful of him,
and he will make straight your paths." – Proverbs 3:6

Most people know when their birthday is, but in Lima, Peru, there can be room for doubt. Cristofer knows this because the official record of his birth is inaccurate. He knows that his mother gave birth to him in Lima on December 12, 1977, because that's what she told him.

"But my father forgot to register me," he said.

He explained that in Lima, when a baby is born, the parents are required to register the child at the civil registry office or face a fine. His father waited two months too long, and so, to avoid paying the penalty, he fudged on the dates. The official record of Cristofer Pereyra's birth says February 12, 1978.

It wasn't the last irresponsible move his father would make. Jose Pereyra was an educated man, trained as a psychologist and a teacher. But he was also a man with a drug problem who left the family—Cristofer, his mother, and his younger brother—when Cristofer was only three years old. He has few memories of his father growing up. The man he identifies with most was one his mother met after his father left.

"Pepe, his name was. He was actually the closest thing to a father figure that I had," he explained. "But not really much of a father figure."

His mother had two daughters with him, and while Pepe didn't stay, Cristofer said his mother raised all of the children together, as one family.

"There is no difference between us, even though they are his daughters," he said.

When Cristofer was 15 years old, the family got word that his grandfather, who was living in the United States, was ill. His mother left the four children with a family friend to go to him, anticipating his death. When he rallied and recovered, she eventually sent for the children, who joined her in Houston, TX, where she enrolled them in school. Cristofer remembers it was not an easy time for him because he spoke almost no English.

"My two high school years in Texas were brutal," he said. "I could have done what a lot of immigrant children do, which is to hang out with the other immigrants. But I could see that the kids in the ESL [English as a Second Language] classes were not people who were ambitious. College was not on their radar. My mom had always instilled in us that we had to go to college to do well in life."

With that in mind, Cristofer took language learning seriously, and within two years, he had begun to master English. But even after enrolling at the University of Houston, he said that while he had a good understanding, he was still very shy about speaking it, especially when he was required to give presentations.

"I don't think I finally felt like I could speak English well until I had my first American girlfriend," he remembered, "because she didn't speak Spanish."

Like most college students, Cristofer was on his own for the first time in his life, and he stuck it out for two years. But in the meantime, his family had moved to Arizona, and he missed them.

"I think I was pretty spoiled. I never really had to fend for myself. My mom still helped me, sent me money, but I held two or three jobs at one time while studying for school, and that went on for two years. But really, ultimately, I just missed them, so I transferred to Arizona State University for no other reason than to live in the same city with them again," he explained.

That decision would turn out to be an important one because it set him up for his first job in public speaking.

"There were a lot of jobs in Arizona, good-paying jobs. I was delivering pizzas at the time and making a lot of money from tips. But I was going to school to be a news reporter. That was my goal. One day, I thought to myself, 'Why am I delivering pizzas when I want to be in the news?' So, I just went into the Univision Station in Phoenix, knocked on the door, and asked, 'Are you hiring for any positions at all? I have zero experience, but I'm happy to do anything.' They had me fill out an application, and a short time later, somebody called me. I was hired as a production assistant with no experience in TV production," Cristofer said.

He didn't know it at the time, but that was his big break into television. That same person who hired him told him later that he was given the job because of his apparent eagerness to learn. And learn he did, from the ground up—setting up lights and microphones, running teleprompter and studio cameras, and perhaps most important, making friends. One of those friends was a woman who did the weather for Univision.

"She was from Colombia. We were both from South America, so we became friends. And one day she told me they were looking for a replacement weather person, and she suggested me. She began coaching me for auditions, and I became the substitute weather guy. After that, I got the chance to do what I really wanted to do, which was reporting—and it ended up being a lot of fun," he recalled.

But he conceded that fun in life isn't necessarily good for the soul.

"This was when I entered what I would think of as my dark night," he said. "Being on TV made me recognized on the streets. For a young 20-something man, that doesn't do a lot of good. That started a period of my life in which I became very superficial and materialistic. I used a lot of people."

It would take quite a while for Cristofer to recognize that part of himself and begin to turn it around.

"I had become a local celebrity, and I don't think I had any more thoughts towards God, because I thought I was almighty and powerful, and I could do anything I wanted," he admitted.

Working in television is a living, but it's not a path to wealth for most people. For that, Cristofer needed a side gig, which he found by selling real estate. He had already purchased his first house, and he decided to get a real estate license and begin to sell. By this time, most of his family members worked as loan officers, and they were able to send business his way. He had become locally famous, and the money was pouring in. What could go wrong?

For one thing, he said he got bored with the television job. Something was nagging at his spirit. He was searching for something, although he wasn't sure what it was. He answered the call by quitting the television job and taking a six-month sabbatical with a trip through South America. He hadn't left the country prior to this and had not gone back to Peru. But now, with a green card in hand, he felt free to travel.

He was drawn to the beauty of the Catholic churches in the towns he drove through. He stayed at guesthouses at many of them, thanks to contacts he'd made with public information officers of Catholic institutions in Phoenix.

"One of them gave me letters of introduction; he got me connections, so I stayed in places that belonged to the Church," he explained.

He noticed the beauty of the churches and appreciated the architecture and the history behind them, but "still, this trip was about having fun, really."

When he returned to Phoenix, he applied for citizenship, and with his finances depleted, it was time to make some money, which wasn't a problem because the real estate market was booming. As he made his rounds one day, he noticed a new recruit—a pretty young loan officer named Karla.

"When I saw her, I was interested right away. Later, what I realized is that God has always drawn me in through beauty. And she had that," he said.

She told him she was a single mom with two kids. They went for coffee, and after that, they kept running into each other. One thing led to another, and before long, Cristofer knew he wanted to make it permanent.

"Because she was Catholic, and more to please her than out of my own interest, I decided to go through the marriage process with her, but it turned out it was really for me," he said.

He said that was the first instance where he began to take a second look at his Catholic faith.

"I went to Confession. I hadn't been to Confession since I was a kid, so I thought, 'Okay, well, maybe this isn't so bad.' I still had issues with the Church because I wasn't well catechized, and I didn't understand many things. I had already consumed a lot of Protestant objections to Catholicism because I'd been exposed more to that, so I had a problem with the statues, with the saints, with Mary, with confessing to a priest—all the typical things. So, going through the marriage program helped me answer a lot of those questions. I saw that there were reasons for all the things that at first, I didn't understand," he said.

The change of heart didn't run deep, though, not at first.

"It began to persuade me gradually, and I remember this thought. 'I know the Catholic Church teaches good morals, so I could use the Catholic Church to raise my children to make sure they have a good moral grounding.' I wanted to manipulate the Church in raising my children, but I wasn't interested in it for me," he said.

And then, the bottom fell out.

"My wife and I went on our honeymoon to Puerto Rico. I was a U.S. citizen, but she didn't have her papers yet. Not a problem, I thought, since Puerto Rico is still the United States and you're not really crossing any borders," he remembered.

They had a good time and came back happy and in love. The woman who stayed with the children while they were away was visiting from Karla's former home in Mexico. They drove her to the bus station with the children so she could return to her village across the border. Cristofer remembers he was relaxed, sitting there in the waiting room reading a newspaper, when he felt a sudden tension in his new wife.

"It happened so fast," he said, "there was barely time to react."

He looked up and saw fear on Karla's face. That's when he noticed the immigration officers walking toward them.

"And they're right there in front of me, and in front of the two little kids, they arrest her. The kids are crying, she's crying, and I was too," he said.

They took Karla into custody, and for three days, Cristofer worked to get a legal team together to get her released. It became a legal battle that went on for years.

"I thought I was in control of everything, but this just brought me to my knees... to the floor. Just this realization that I can control nothing. That began an ordeal that, by the grace of God and another miracle, we were able to resolve so she wasn't sent back to Mexico," he said.

But there were more storm clouds on the horizon. As the new family was dealing with the immigration problem, the recession hit, and the real estate market dried up. Cristofer owned three houses starting out in his marriage, one they were living in and two he had as investment rentals. Suddenly, nobody was buying houses, and his commissions were no longer covering his expenses. Before long, he couldn't manage his mortgages. He ended up having to sell all three properties and had to move his family into a rental unit. Unable to survive by selling real estate, he instead opened an insurance agency, but that, too, was slow going. Within months, his perfect life had fallen down around him.

"It definitely put me in my place," he said. "I finally understood who I was. I understood I was not in control, and that's when I began to look for God."

Out of other options, Cristofer began taking his young family to church.

A Meeting That Would Change His Life

When we are open and asking for help, the Holy Spirit will step up, often putting someone in our path who can make all the difference. For Cristofer, that person was his pastor, Fr. Alonso Saenz.

"I consider him a saint," he said. "Every Sunday, I would walk away just immersed in thought, digesting everything he said. I started hearing for the first time about holiness. I had gone to a few Catholic Masses, but I hadn't heard about living in holiness anywhere. It was a recurring theme [from Fr. Saenz]. Holiness in our ordinary lives, right where we are. That thought resonated with me.

"I began consuming a lot of apologetics, videos, and books, and began teaching myself the faith. I didn't have any formal religious education, but through my seven years of running the insurance agency, during my off times, I fell in love with catechesis, starting with Pope Benedict XVI. I read all the encyclicals from his pontificate from the beginning. Once I realized how good they were, I started reading everything that was published on the Vatican website, all the magisterial documents from Benedict.

"I remember learning at that point that he was one of the people who was a close advisor to Pope John Paul II. I thought if Benedict was that good, I bet John Paul was also good, and I started reading him—every document, every encyclical, everything. And then I realized that the *Catechism of the Catholic Church* had been published during Pope John Paul II's time, but under the oversight of Pope Benedict XVI. I read the whole thing, and then I read the Bible, front to back."

One of the things he learned by reading the encyclicals was that it was not enough to know a lot about the faith; he also had to persevere in charity and change how he was living his life. At about that time, Cristofer remembers learning about Opus Dei and St. Josemaria Escriva, and he was drawn to the message of living a life of everyday holiness. He began reading about it and felt that it simply made sense. He began following its practices—to attend daily Mass and make time for regular Adoration and Confession.

"They take the call seriously to dedicate their lives to striving for holiness in everything they do," he said, "from the simplest, most mundane activity through the highest-level career tasks; whatever they do, they offer it up to God. It works for everybody, right where they are."

As Cristofer learned more about the Catholic faith, he went on retreats, visited often with Fr. Saenz, all while selling insurance. One day, a friend reached out to tell him he was starting up a Catholic radio station in Phoenix, and knowing of his background in media and his interest in his newfound faith, he wondered if Cristofer would like to be involved.

"So, I was a radio talk show host for five years— one of those shows people would listen to on their morning commute. And after the radio show, I'd go in and open the business. That was my routine, Monday to Friday," he said.

One day, he received a call from Bishop Olmsted, who had heard him on the radio and wanted to meet him, so he invited him to lunch. A friendship developed between the two, and when a new position opened in the Phoenix Diocese Mission office, Cristofer considered applying.

"At that point, my insurance business was finally taking off," he said. "But I went to my wife and told her, 'This is the job I never knew I wanted,' because now I had a thirst for the faith, and there in front of me was a job description that looked a lot like my background. I thought, 'If it's God's will, I'll apply and see what happens.' They offered me the job."

On his first day with the Diocese, Cristofer remembers asking the bishop what he would most like to see accomplished. Bishop Olmsted said that in five years, he wanted Cristofer to have identified who the leaders were in the community and see them brought closer to the Church.

"Well, at first, I was thinking very much in terms of Hispanic Catholics, because that was my role," he explained. "But after a year, I was sent as a representative of the Diocese of Phoenix to a secular leadership program, and it was that experience that ignited in me the desire to start Tepeyac Leadership Initiative."

He said he could see the value in the methodology used in the secular program and in the way it was taught, but in terms of the message, he simply wasn't sold.

"It was awful in terms of the values they were promoting," he said. "I remember thinking, 'We could do this, and we could do it better because we could make it Catholic.' I went to the bishop and pitched him my idea. I was still thinking Hispanic mission, but he said do it for the whole Diocese, and that's how we developed TLI."

It started small at first, with participants within the greater Phoenix area, but Cristofer said God and Bishop Olmsted had a different plan.

"We realized in about the third year that this was something the whole Church needed, and the bishop had already given a green light to making it an independent 501c3 nonprofit organization. I was already reaching out to dioceses in Los Angeles, preparing to take it to one diocese at a time. The Phoenix Diocese was basically paying my salary while I was developing a new organization with the support of the bishop and the leadership, and then... Covid happened... and everybody panicked," he said.

As happened everywhere, people began staying home, donations dropped off, budgets tightened up, people were furloughed, and Cristofer was laid off.

"The Chancellor said when she let me go that she was sorry, that the Bishop supported me, that they all supported me, but they could just no longer keep me on the payroll. She said she hoped there would be a way for TLI to continue. So, I thought, 'What now?' And this was a God moment. I suddenly realized I already had a board, and it was a pretty smart group of people, so I called them together. I remember my wife and children were waiting outside because they knew I was going to pitch something important, and that our future depended on the outcome of that meeting. They were silently listening to my conversation on Zoom. I basically said it's time to have some skin in the game," he said.

Up until that moment, he explained, the board didn't have a funding commitment. They were purely contributing their ideas but were not asked to contribute monetarily, as is customary for most boards, because up until then, there had been no need. Now, suddenly, there was. The board voted to ask for a fundraising commitment from all 10 members, raising enough money in five minutes to keep going for a few more months. Following that, the Diocese contributed grant money to keep the program alive.

"God had given me a parachute," he said. "He really gave me a sense of optimism, and I knew if I keep trusting, He's going to be there."

That trust has been pivotal because money is always tight.

"We've never been more than six months ahead," he added, "but somehow, we always get through it. I just need to keep trusting."

He also points out the unforeseen benefits brought about by Covid. Prior to the pandemic, the idea of virtual meetings was there, but it happened only occasionally. After people were isolated, it became the norm, so Cristofer's idea of traveling to one diocese at a time no longer applied.

"That would have taken forever," he realized. "The pandemic forced us to either shut the program down or go virtual. We thought we wouldn't like the virtual option. We thought it was beneath us, that it would diminish the quality of the experience."

But not only has that not been the case, it has allowed the program to grow exponentially.

"When we were forced to go virtual, it opened the doors to the world. Shortly thereafter, we had people from all over the world participating. This year, in June, we're going to have graduated 400 people, from every continent," he said.

Surrender is still a part of Cristofer's daily life. In the corporate world, he acknowledges he would likely be in some corner office with a secure financial future, but he said that would not be living out the call to holiness as he sees it. When he closes his eyes at night, he said he can give thanks because he has a lot to be grateful for.

It took years to unravel his wife's legal problems, but that trauma is now behind them. Their children are doing well, and he is close with his extended family. He acknowledged they don't necessarily share his faith walk, but they respect him for the work he does, and they support him in it. These days, he said he doesn't spend a lot of time worrying about what tomorrow will bring. He acknowledges that he's as flawed as the next guy, but he does his best to work toward sainthood while he can, and a perfect day means he's helping to bring others along for the ride.

As he puts it, "We can't win souls for Christ if we don't first win our own. The rest follows."

Appendix A

2025 Interview with Cristofer Pereyra, Founder and CEO of Tepeyac Leadership, Inc.

The Church is not without problems. When faced with them, many people choose to simply leave the Church. What do you say to those people?

The first chapter of my book [*Catholic Leadership for Civil Society*] is titled "Don't leave, lead." The real problem we have at hand is a lack of identity in the faithful. If we feel confident about our Divine filiation, if we know we are children of God, no matter how bad things get, we know we are on the winning side. Those problems we are so frustrated with do not occur in spite of God. Nothing happens if God doesn't will it or allow it. It's a mystery, because the next question is "Why does God allow it?" But our focus should be on being faithful through the storm. God is allowing the storm. What is He saying to us as a Church? What is He saying to me? How do you want me to respond to this, Lord? That's where our attitude should be. Our hope and trust are in the Lord. The battle is won. We must simply be faithful.

On the flip side, people who have a reawakening to their faith often become hyper-involved in parish work. But that's not the main message of TLI, is it?

Absolutely not. TLI has set out to change the chip in the minds of lay Catholic men and women to help them rediscover the authentic character of the lay vocation. We are not meant to set up a tent and camp out at the parish. We must absolutely be of service to our pastors and involved in our parish community, but our field of mission as lay people is the world.

Giving of one's treasure is important, but we are also asked to give of our time and talent. Is one more important than the other when it comes to evangelization?

I would say prayer is the most important thing. Second comes talent and then treasure. Every battle in this world is first fought within. Lay Catholics need to rediscover the depths of the interior life. That's where our strength comes from. And this can only be done through a committed plan of spiritual life. When we are grounded in prayer, our gifts and talents are multiplied and, in a way, enhanced. What we have to give then in terms of treasure is very circumstantial, in my opinion. God has blessed some with more or less abundance of resources, according to their own state in life and God's will for them. If you have more, by all means, give more. Those who have in abundance have a duty to give in abundance. The rest of us can give what we can.

You talk a lot about the forgotten call from Vatican II. Can you elaborate on what that means for today's Catholics?

I travel all over giving talks on Catholic leadership for civil society. I often ask audiences to raise their hand if they have heard about Vatican II. Then, I ask them to keep their hands up if they have read any documents from Vatican II. Until this day, we talk a lot about the Second Vatican Council, and most Catholics focus primarily on the changes that came about in the liturgy and the ecumenical aspects of the Council. But by far, most people miss the mark on the bold, urgent challenge that the council had for the laity. Vatican II gave the laity, for the first time with such a boldness and clarity, its marching orders. It told us who we were as laity in the Church and in the world. Our mission is to transform society from within. Not even the Pope can do that in the way the laity is positioned to do it, precisely because of our state in life. We must insert ourselves in the secular fabric of society as to sanctify it from within.

What qualities make up a successful lay Catholic leader?

Service. Leadership is service. A servant heart is the heart of a leader. The rest are details, and there are plenty of qualities, virtues, and skills that leaders should have, but it all starts with service. Every baptized Catholic is called to lead others to Christ. By virtue of our Baptism, we are all called to lead. The way we lead is by inspiring others, bringing out the greatness in them. This is accomplished best by serving them. The ultimate example of leadership is Christ himself, who didn't come to be served but to serve others.

Are there particular areas in our society today that are crying out for more Catholic leaders to step up?

Certainly—education, healthcare, business, government, immigration, news media, and the list goes on. But there is one field that offers the broadest opportunity to lead. It encompasses all areas of secular life. Behind every human institution, there's a group of people who come together on a regular basis to enact policies and chart the direction of that organization. That is a board. Board service is where leadership happens. Well-formed, faithful, and committed Catholics must have a seat at every table where decisions are made.

Can you talk more about why that's an important part of the TLI mission?

When a well-formed Catholic serves on a board, everyone wins. The institution he or she is serving gains insights and expertise from the board member. The community and those being served by the institution are benefiting from the insights and expertise of the board member, and everyone gains. The Church gains a voice, a seat at a table where important decisions are made. And last, the board member gains experience, grows his network, and often encounters new professional opportunities through board service.

Appendix B

2025 Interview with Most Reverend Thomas J. Olmsted, Bishop Emeritus of Phoenix, AZ

Bishop, TLI is trying to form leaders who are eager to bring their Catholic faith into the public square. But leadership and servant leadership are two very different things. How can an individual tell when he or she is following God's plan as opposed to their own?

Leaders in the Church build their lives on the love of Jesus that came to life in their hearts through Baptism, and that comes to fruition wherever the Holy Spirit leads them. Lay persons play an irreplaceable role in the life and mission of the Church through marriage and family life, responsible citizenship, leadership in cultural and professional life, and fidelity to what is good and just in the public square.

That doesn't mean to be a leader one has to go through painful experiences, but I think we can all agree that following Jesus necessitates acceptance of suffering should it come. Have you had any experiences of surrender that you're willing to share that might help to illustrate the points you're making?

Public witness to the Gospel requires love, truth, humility, and courage—virtues badly needed when defending the most vulnerable among us, promoting their dignity and right to life, standing for freedom of conscience and freedom of religion, and cultivating unity and charity during times of strife.

On some occasions of my life as a bishop, I have been asked to assume pastoral leadership in the face of crises. I would not have volunteered at those times, but agreed to say "Yes," trusting in the grace of obedience. If the Lord calls us to do something, He will give us the grace to complete it.

Fulfillment of our duties in the public square requires close communion with Christ, ongoing formation in the social teaching of the Church, and a constantly renewed commitment to the works of mercy and the Gospel of life.

Lay Catholics, like Religious and Clergy, invite the Lord to do with them whatever He wills, not worrying about public opinion but surrendering all into His hands. God knows what is best for us; He is worthy of our trust. Jesus promises, "Whoever remains in me and I in him will bear much fruit, because without me you can do nothing." (John 15:5)

We need not know "when" He is at work in us or "when" He is at work in others. Jesus makes all things work together for the good; let us leave it all in His hands (Cf. Matthew 25:31-46). Every day, I pray the prayer of St. Charles de Foucauld: "Father, I abandon myself into your hands, do with me what you will; whatever you may do, I thank you, I am ready for all, I accept all. Let only your work be done in me and in all your creatures."

Through Baptism, we are called to live our faith in the Lord, trust Him day in and day out, in public or in private, at our job or our profession, when healthy or when ill, whether popular or not. We thank God for whatever He does, for whatever He permits to happen, for being the Lord and Master of our lives.

How do we know when to persevere on our own with a problem and when to just surrender that problem to God? It can be especially hard for people who consider that to be "giving up."

I seek to surrender every part of my day to the Lord, beginning with that prayer of abandonment. My days are made up of various projects; some can be addressed at once, others require study and extended time. Still others require consultation and collaboration. Prioritizing the projects helps me to be productive and keep a balanced perspective on the problem at hand.

Do you think our own stubbornness prevents God from being able to accomplish His work through us?

Yes, discipleship begins with conversion, metanoia, a change of mind and heart aided by the mercy of God. We often need to persevere in order to fulfill God's will, but it never helps to insist on doing it my way. God's plan trumps our own. He knows what He is about. Trust Him.

Because people like cowboys or Navy Seals are tough and loath to show weakness, they can find servant leadership challenging, since traditional leadership can seem to be about power or dominance. How can strong people change this perception so that the focus is on caring for and guiding others rather than controlling them? After all, I don't think anybody would argue that Jesus was weak.

Jesus tells us, "Unless you change and become like children, you cannot enter the Kingdom of God." He also said, "Unless you take up your cross each day and follow me, you cannot enter the Kingdom of God." A faith-filled perspective can be cultivated by returning often to the words that Jesus told us to pray. "Father, Thy Kingdom come: Thy will be done..."

Do you think there's a difference in the way men and women lead?

No two leaders are exactly alike. Good leaders succeed because they collaborate well, recognize the God-given gifts of their colleagues, and do not worry about who gets the credit for success.

Concluding Prayer

The Surrender Novena

Given by Jesus to Servant of God Fr. Dolindo Ruotolo (1882-1970)

Day 1

Why do you confuse yourselves by worrying? Leave the care of your affairs to me and everything will be peaceful. I say to you in truth that every act of true, blind, complete surrender to me produces the effect that you desire and resolves all difficult situations.

O Jesus, I surrender myself to you, take care of everything! (10 times)

Day 2

Surrender to me does not mean to fret, to be upset, or to lose hope, nor does it mean offering to me a worried prayer asking me to follow you and change your worry into prayer. It is against this surrender, deeply against it, to worry, to be nervous and to desire to think about the consequences of anything. It is like the confusion that children feel when they ask their mother to see to their needs, and then try to take care of those needs for themselves so that their childlike efforts get in their mother's way. Surrender means to placidly close the eyes of the soul, to turn away from thoughts of tribulation and to put yourself in my care, so that only I act, saying, "You take care of it."

O Jesus, I surrender myself to you, take care of everything! (10 times)

Day 3

How many things I do when the soul, in so much spiritual and material need, turns to me, looks at me and says to me, "You take care of it," then closes its eyes and rests. In pain you pray for me to act, but that I act in the way you want. You do not turn to me, instead, you want me to adapt to your ideas. You are not sick people who ask the doctor to cure you, but rather sick people who tell the doctor how to. So do not act this way, but pray as I taught you in the Our Father: "Hallowed be thy Name," that is, be glorified in my need. "Thy kingdom come," that is, let all that is in us and in the world be in accord with your kingdom. "Thy will be done on Earth as it is in Heaven," that is, in our need, decide as you see fit for our temporal and eternal life. If you say to me truly: "Thy will be done," which is the same as saying: "You take care of it," I will intervene with all my omnipotence, and I will resolve the most difficult situations.

O Jesus, I surrender myself to you, take care of everything! (10 times)

Day 4

You see evil growing instead of weakening? Do not worry. Close your eyes and say to me with faith: "Thy will be done, You take care of it." I say to you that I will take care of it, and that I will intervene as does a doctor and I will accomplish miracles when they are needed. Do you see that the sick person is getting worse? Do not be upset, but close your eyes and say, "You take care of it." I say to you that I will take care of it, and that there is no medicine more powerful than my loving intervention. By my love, I promise this to you.

O Jesus, I surrender myself to you, take care of everything! (10 times)

Day 5

And when I must lead you on a path different from the one you see, I will prepare you; I will carry you in my arms; I will let you find yourself, like children who have fallen asleep in their mother's arms, on the other bank of the river. What troubles you and hurts you immensely are your reason, your thoughts and worry, and your desire at all costs to deal with what afflicts you.

O Jesus, I surrender myself to you, take care of everything! (10 times)

Day 6

You are sleepless; you want to judge everything, direct everything and see to everything and you surrender to human strength, or worse—to men themselves, trusting in their intervention—this is what hinders my words and my views. Oh, how much I wish from you this surrender, to help you; and how I suffer when I see you so agitated! Satan tries to do exactly this: to agitate you and to remove you from my protection and to throw you into the jaws of human initiative. So, trust only in me, rest in me, surrender to me in everything.

O Jesus, I surrender myself to you, take care of everything! (10 times)

Day 7

I perform miracles in proportion to your full surrender to me and to your not thinking of yourselves. I sow treasure troves of graces when you are in the deepest poverty. No person of reason, no thinker, has ever performed miracles, not even among the saints. He does divine works whosoever surrenders to God. So don't think about it any more, because your mind is acute and for you it is very hard to see evil and to trust in me and to not think of yourself. Do this for all your needs, do this, all of you, and you will see great continual silent

miracles. I will take care of things, I promise this to you.

O Jesus, I surrender myself to you, take care of everything! (10 times)

Day 8

Close your eyes and let yourself be carried away on the flowing current of my grace; close your eyes and do not think of the present, turning your thoughts away from the future just as you would from temptation. Repose in me, believing in my goodness, and I promise you by my love that if you say, "You take care of it," I will take care of it all; I will console you, liberate you and guide you.

O Jesus, I surrender myself to you, take care of everything! (10 times)

Day 9

Pray always in readiness to surrender, and you will receive from it great peace and great rewards, even when I confer on you the grace of immolation, of repentance, and of love. Then what does suffering matter? It seems impossible to you? Close your eyes and say with all your soul, "Jesus, you take care of it." Do not be afraid, I will take care of things and you will bless my name by humbling yourself. A thousand prayers cannot equal one single act of surrender, remember this well. There is no novena more effective than this.

O Jesus, I surrender myself to you, take care of everything! (10 times)

Mother, I am yours
now and forever.
Through you and with you
I always want to belong
completely to Jesus.

We hope you enjoyed this book.
Please consider supporting our efforts by learning about,
praying for, or financially supporting
Tepeyac Leadership, Inc.

Please visit:
TLIprogram.org
THLconference.org

Monica Hannan is an Emmy-Award-winning journalist who has authored several books, including *The Dream Maker* and *Gift of Death*. She has a Bachelor's degree in History from Minnesota State University Moorhead, a Master's in Management degree from the University of Mary, and a Master of Theology degree from the Augustine Institute. She is married to Cliff Naylor and they have three adult children.

www.ingramcontent.com/pod-product-compliance
Lightning Source LLC
Chambersburg PA
CBHW060630130626
46555CB00002B/742